AFRICAN CONFLICT RESOLUTION

The U.S. Role in Peacemaking

D1450751

AFRICAN
CONFLICT
RESOLUTION

The U.S. Role in Peacemaking

David R. Smock and
Chester A. Crocker
Editors

United States Institute of Peace Press
Washington, D.C.

United States Institute of Peace
1550 M Street NW, Suite 700
Washington, DC 20005–1708

First published 1995

Printed in the United States of America

The paper used in this publication meets the minimum requirements of American National Standard for Information Sciences—Permanence of Paper for Printed Library Materials, ANSI Z39.48–1984.

Library of Congress Cataloging-in-Publication Data
African conflict resolution: the U.S. role in peacemaking / David R. Smock and
   Chester A. Crocker, editors.
     p. cm.
   Includes bibliographical references and index.
   ISBN 1-878379-00-3
    1. Conflict management—Africa. 2. Violence—Africa. 3. United States—
Foreign relations—Africa. 4. Africa—Foreign relations—United States. I.
Smock, David R. II. Crocker, Chester A.
   JX1961.A35A33 1995
   327.7306—dc20   95-19963
                                                    CIP

CONTENTS

AFRICAN CONFLICT RESOLUTION

The U.S. Role in Peacemaking

1

INTRODUCTION

David R. Smock

On September 28, 1994, the United States Institute of Peace brought together forty specialists from Africa and the United States—including former and current diplomats, academics, U.S. policymakers, and policy analysts—to discuss ways to improve the U.S. contribution to African efforts to prevent, manage, and resolve violent conflicts. The purposes of the discussion were to (1) assess lessons learned from past U.S. peacemaking efforts in Africa; (2) gauge the capacity of African states, regional organizations, and nongovernmental organizations (NGOs) to take more responsibility for peacemaking; (3) assess what outside assistance could enable African institutions to be more effective peacemakers; and (4) consider the U.S. role in conflict resolution in Africa.

This book is the product of that symposium. Its major recommendation is that the United States continue active engagement with Africa and creatively support African initiatives to manage and resolve African conflicts. Africa has a new willingness to assume responsibility for peacemaking, but its institutional and financial capabilities are limited. African initiatives have no chance of success in promoting greater peace without significant and sustained international, and particularly American, involvement.

The 1992 U.S. intervention in Somalia and the failure of the subsequent United Nations (UN) effort to build a new state in that war-ravaged country might be viewed as a turning point in U.S. involvement in African conflicts. The widely publicized deaths of U.S. and other peacekeeping troops at the hands of Somali militiamen hardened attitudes among American policymakers and the public about the efficacy and costs of U.S. military intervention. A mood of "Afro-pessimism" and "conflict fatigue" has prevailed since then.

Most Africa analysts agree that the United States will probably continue to be engaged in African conflict resolution—where U.S. national interests are real but not always apparent—and will generally be guided by the principle of "African solutions to African problems." But, as noted by National Security Adviser Anthony Lake in an address to the Organization of African Unity (OAU) in December 1994, "Those of us who recognize the importance of continued active engagement and support for Africa are confronting the reality of shrinking resources and an honest skepticism about the return on our investments in peacekeeping and development."[1]

Given this wariness about military engagement in Africa following the experience in Somalia, what options does the United States have to strengthen the capacity of Africans to resolve conflicts within or between African states? How should the U.S. government and American NGOs contribute to conflict resolution in Africa? These are the issues addressed in this volume, and they are addressed by American and African scholars, policy analysts, and former high-ranking officials.

One can point to notable successes in international efforts to achieve peace in Africa, including South Africa, Namibia, and Mozambique, but devastating conflicts still plague the continent. Sixteen African nations are involved in some form of civil conflict, spawning an estimated 6 to 7 million refugees, close to half of the world's refugee total. An additional 17 million Africans are internally displaced, in most cases because of civil wars. Since the 1960s, the countries of sub-Saharan Africa have suffered from deadly conflict to a greater degree than any other world region except Southeast Asia.

Prospects for the future are not promising. A U.S. Central Intelligence Agency (CIA) intelligence estimate prepared at the end of 1994 reportedly stated, "In the next 12 to 18 months, ethnic conflict, civil war, and natural disasters will place a greater demand on humanitarian support in Africa than at any time since the 1960s." This estimate depicts sub-Saharan Africa as the "most strife-torn region in the world" and anticipates that 30 million people there may be at risk of malnutrition or death in 1995 if emergency aid is not provided. Five African nations—Zaire, Sudan, Liberia, Sierra Leone, and Somalia—are in danger of complete collapse, and Nigeria, Chad, and Mali are listed as "trouble spots . . . where major factional fighting could break out" in 1995.[2] In January 1995 *Africa Confidential* concluded that the nation-state is losing its grip in Africa because of unstable borders, large refugee flows between states, massive international migration within Africa, civil strife, criminal cross-border trading networks, the emergence of warlords in several countries, and foreign intervention.[3]

African states spend $8 billion annually on their militaries, scarce resources that could more productively be spent improving the African standard of living. Significant steps have been taken in some countries to reduce the size and expense of armies. Such countries as Mozambique, Ethiopia, Eritrea, Uganda, and Namibia have made impressive progress in dismantling their war machines and reintegrating the combatants into civilian society or into scaled-down national armies.

Dating back to the time of the UN intervention in the Congo in the 1960s, the United States has made a significant commitment to peace-making in Africa. This involvement has grown over the past fifteen years. The United States took the lead in the mediation process that gave Namibia its independence and removed Cuban and South African troops from Angola. The United States also has been successfully engaged in peacemaking processes in Zimbabwe, Mozambique, Angola, Ethiopia, Eritrea, and South Africa. U.S. assistance also has helped sustain the peace-keeping and mediation efforts of the Economic Community of West African States (ECOWAS) in Liberia. Recent large-scale American involvements, including use of American troops, occurred in Somalia and Rwanda.

American interventions to resolve African conflicts before 1992 did not arouse much domestic public attention or debate, because they generally were relatively inexpensive and did not engage American ground troops. But the involvement of large numbers of U.S. troops in Somalia raised public awareness and anxiety to a new height. Moreover, budget cutters have pointed to the annual average of $1.5 billion that the U.S. government spends on relief operations in Africa, mostly in countries suffering from civil wars.

As Herman Cohen writes later in this book, increasing caution toward major commitment of American resources to international peacemaking and peacekeeping began in 1992 after the price tag of the Cambodia operation was announced. Then the American humanitarian intervention in Somalia in December 1992 generated a new level of American awareness of and involvement in Africa's wars. Television images of mass starvation and intimidation of women and children aroused compassion and laid the basis for impressive public support for American intervention. But unrealistic expectations led the public to believe that the American-led international force could not only save millions of Somalis from starvation but could also return Somalia to the path of peace and stability. Although many lives were saved, several factors conspired to make the mission much more difficult than the public had expected. The Somali warlords proved intransigent; the goal of peace- and nation-building proved to be extraordinarily complex in a sociopolitical situation that few outsiders comprehended; and U.S.-UN policy took a wrong turn in the summer of 1993 when operations became fixated on arresting General Mohamed Aideed.

The killing of eighteen American Rangers on October 3, 1993, and the dramatic television pictures of the body of an American being dragged through the streets of Mogadishu dramatically undercut public and congressional support for the American and UN missions in Somalia, and forced a rethinking of future U.S. international commitments to peacemaking and peacekeeping. President Clinton quickly announced that U.S. troops would be withdrawn from Somalia by March 1994.

In September 1993, in a speech on peacekeeping to the UN General Assembly, Clinton stated, "The United Nations must know when to say no." Work was initiated on a new set of policy guidelines, embodied in Presidential Decision Directive 25 (PDD 25), to govern U.S. involvement in UN-sponsored peacekeeping and peacemaking. The policy, published in May 1994, articulated a set of criteria for deciding which peace operations the United States should support and participate in. PDD 25 established a checklist of questions, including whether UN involvement would advance U.S. interests; whether the objectives and mission are clearly understood; whether realistic criteria for ending the operation are in place; whether U.S. military personnel would be at risk; whether U.S. participation is essential to success; whether prospects are good for public and congressional support; whether there is a plan and a commitment to achieve a decisive outcome; and whether an endgame can be explicitly identified. Taken as a whole the criteria are so demanding that they read like a rationale to excuse American inaction. Some viewed the new policy as a justification for American neglect of future crises in Africa. The unfortunate lesson drawn from the American-led UN intervention in Somalia was that in the future such large-scale interventions should be avoided. The fact that the mission, despite all the difficulties and mistakes, saved hundreds of thousands of lives has largely been ignored.

The first major test of the new U.S. policy in Africa came with the Rwanda crisis in April 1994, when the genocidal slaughters commenced. Unfortunately for Rwanda, it did not meet the tougher test for intervention set down after Somalia. In June 1994, Herman Cohen, former assistant secretary of state for African affairs, described the U.S. reaction to Rwanda in this fashion: "American policy on Rwanda is difficult to understand. Statements made by Madeleine Albright, the U.S. ambassador to the United Nations, indicate that Rwanda is viewed as a traditional peacekeeping problem, when it is really a 'Call 911!' problem. Rwanda . . . is a case of planned, systematic murder of men, women, and children who happen to belong to a particular group—the Tutsi. . . . The administration sees no vital American interest engaged in Rwanda, and therefore does not want UN troops to have a muscular mandate even though African troops would be willing to take on such a difficult and dangerous assignment."[4] Serious delays were later encountered in providing equipment to African troops prepared and authorized to enter Rwanda. Moreover, U.S. officials were very reluctant to call the slaughter of half a million Tutsis "genocide" because such a declaration would have obliged a more active UN and U.S. intervention. The United States later welcomed France's unilateral intervention to establish safe havens for displaced Rwandans.

Roger Winter, director of the U.S. Committee for Refugees, wrote this after a visit to Rwanda in June 1994: "The United States whines that it cannot be a global policeman and that this nation is too exhausted to supply troops to halt genocide—this despite the fact that the 69,545 UN troops currently on peacekeeping assignments worldwide include only 867 Americans. If America chooses to turn its back on Rwanda, it cannot be because this nation is overstretched by the burden of supplying 1 percent of the UN's peacekeepers."[5]

Despite such strong criticism, the Clinton administration held firm against military intervention to stop the slaughter, although the United States has provided significant humanitarian assistance to Rwandan refugees. It was one of the first nations to begin flying relief supplies to Rwandan refugee camps in Tanzania. A major relief effort continues to the Rwandan refugee camps in Zaire, and 2,350 American troops were used to help deliver water, food, and sanitation to refugees in Zaire as well as to facilitate the return of refugees to Rwanda.

As the United States has grown less willing to intervene in Africa's wars, the OAU and some African regional organizations have indicated preparedness to shoulder more responsibility for Africa's peacemaking. Mention has already been made of the substantial contribution that the ECOWAS states have made since 1990 to restoring peace in Liberia, after the United States failed to take the lead there. Troops have been provided, principally by Nigeria and Ghana, and innumerable mediation sessions have been assembled in an effort to find a formula for peace among Liberia's several warring factions. Starting in 1994 the regional organization for East Africa, IGADD (Intergovernmental Authority on Drought and Development), has hosted and facilitated negotiating sessions between the government in Khartoum and the rebel forces from southern Sudan to try to end Sudan's devastating civil war.

At the OAU summit in June 1992, African heads of state agreed that the OAU should establish "a mechanism for preventing, managing, and resolving conflicts in Africa." At the 1993 summit the heads of state formally approved the mechanism as it was proposed by the OAU secretary-general. Rather remarkably for an organization that hitherto has avoided involvement in internal conflicts, the new OAU mechanism has a clear mandate to concern itself with such conflicts. The mechanism is charged with anticipating and preventing conflicts, as well as engaging in peacekeeping and peacebuilding activities.

The commitment of African heads of state to the OAU initiative is impressive and promises new energy in addressing Africa's wars, but it is also clear that the mechanism will for some time be a weak instrument on which to pin hopes for a peaceful Africa. The OAU needs substantial assistance in training staff, developing systems, and financing peacemaking operations. James Gustave Speth, administrator of the United Nations Development Program (UNDP), has advocated establishing an African Peace Fund to which donors would contribute up to $300 to $400 million to assist the OAU's peacemaking program. Speth points out that this would represent only 10 percent of the $3 to $4 billion that the international community has already spent on conflict resolution in Africa.[6]

At a speech to the White House Conference on Africa in June 1994, Salim A. Salim, secretary-general of the OAU, called for a partnership to promote peace in Africa. He pointed to the OAU's new conflict resolution mechanism as an indication of "Africa's new resolve to take the mantle of leadership" in addressing its conflicts. Salim also said that only through taking initiative will Africa deserve external assistance for its efforts. Setting up the mechanism is part of Africa's effort to "wean itself from the dependence syndrome.... We see in the continent greater realism and preparedness to depart from established habits of blaming others for its ills and of looking to outsiders for their resolution." Although Africa will assume new responsibility, it will still need outside support and assistance of various kinds, with the United States taking the lead.[7]

The Clinton administration and Congress seem prepared to provide some support for African peacemaking initiatives. In 1994 the United States gave the OAU $3.3 million to strengthen its peacekeeping and peacemaking operations. Additional funds have been earmarked to provide equipment and training to enable African states to participate in international and regional peacekeeping endeavors. Aid is also being provided for military demobilization in countries like Uganda and Ethiopia.

In October 1994 President Clinton signed the African Conflict Resolution Act of 1994, which originated in the Africa subcommittee of the House Foreign Affairs Committee. This act authorizes $1.5 million annually for FY 1995 to FY 1998 to assist the OAU's conflict resolution program. An additional $25 million is authorized in 1995 and 1996 to pay for the demobilization and reintegration of African military personnel into civilian societies.

Deputy Secretary of State Strobe Talbott led an American delegation to five African countries in October 1994 to explore how the United States could strengthen African peacekeeping capability. Talbott was quoted as saying, "There is no shortage of African countries willing to take part in peacekeeping efforts," but they don't have the capacity to do it on their own.[8]

Similar sentiments have been voiced elsewhere. At the summit of francophone states hosted by France in November 1994, the French indicated that they are tiring of their traditional role as the region's gendarme, and they encouraged African leaders to organize a standing peacekeeping force. "The time has come for Africans themselves to resolve their conflicts and organize their own security," stated French President Francois Mitterrand.[9] The African leaders present recognized that continued reliance on intervention by France or other western powers was unrealistic, but they foresaw enormous political, logistical, and financial obstacles to creating a standing force of peacekeepers.

The most far-reaching proposals to guide African states in assuming responsibility for security and peacemaking in Africa are in the Kampala Declaration, formulated under the sponsorship of the Africa Leadership Forum in 1991. This declaration, prepared at a gathering of 500 African leaders, called for a conference on security, stability, development, and cooperation in Africa (CSSDCA). CSSDCA would be expected to organize continental peacekeeping machinery and initiate confidence-building measures and nonaggression pacts among all African states.[10] These proposals were introduced at the OAU summit in 1992, but they were too radical to permit quick adoption or implementation.

In 1994, the World Bank-assisted Global Coalition for Africa (GCA) proposed the creation of a conflict prevention network in Africa to be known as Africa Reconciliation to be jointly sponsored by the OAU and the GCA. Africa Reconciliation would organize an early warning system for developing crises and maintain a network of volunteer mediators and intervenors who would provide good offices in an effort to reduce tensions and defuse confrontational political situations.

This book, in an effort to advance consideration of these issues, includes the papers presented at the Institute's September 1994 symposium and summarizes the discussion and debate. Chapters 2 and 3 offer the perspectives of two leading Africans. The second chapter, by Ali Mazrui, diagnoses some of the major sources of civil conflict in Africa and speculates about actions that Africans, African states, and African organizations might take to promote peace. In chapter 3 B. A. Kiplagat emphasizes the importance of early warning and preventive diplomacy, by both African NGOs and African governments, in heading off conflict and the fundamental role that civil society and strong democratic institutions can play in helping to resolve future African conflicts. The next two chapters assess American experience in trying to resolve African conflicts and draw lessons for the future from these cases. Donald Rothchild offers a scholarly analysis of these issues in chapter 4, while Robert Oakley provides a diplomatic perspective in chapter 5. Chapter 6, by Herman Cohen, assesses African potential and recommends specific U.S. actions and policies. In chapter 7 William Zartman provides some guidelines for preserving peace in Africa. In chapter 8 Timothy Sisk summarizes the symposium discussion and delineates the recommendations that emerged from that discussion. A concluding chapter by Chester Crocker offers recommendations for American policy, based on an overview of the papers and the discussion.[11]

2

THE AFRICAN STATE AS A POLITICAL REFUGEE

Ali A. Mazrui

The African state shares characteristics with the refugees it helps to create.[1] Most African states are artificial, and both the states and the refugees are fundamentally without roots. The rootlessness and artificiality of the African state are attributable to its colonial origins and its artificial boundaries. The rootlessness of individual refugees is based on the postcolonial political traumas of disruption and displacement.

One issue that faces both states and refugees is that of alienation. Both the African state and individual refugees are often alienated from the societies in which they find themselves. This alienation can be morally unsettling and can distort the ethics and standards of behavior of the refugees and of those in control of the state. What is right and what is wrong, what is bad and what is good, can undergo disconcerting mutations under the pressure of "refugee flows." Is the twenty-first century the time to undertake new ways of solving the crisis of the African state and of ameliorating and decreasing the refugee crisis in Africa?

In global terms the African state has become increasingly marginalized and has been pushed into the ghetto of the world system. Like Africa's refugees, many African states were already living, at least partly, on handouts before the 1990s. But the international community has become weary of appeals for charity. Further, the end of the Cold War has diverted western investment and aid toward the former members of the Warsaw Pact and the newly liberalizing economies of China, Vietnam, and India. The new priorities of the post–Cold War era are, to some extent, bad news for disabled African states and displaced African people. In addition, the francophone economies have lost the financial asylum they used to enjoy from the French franc. From now on francophone African countries may have to deal with the full rigors of state formation, including the danger of producing economic and even political refugees, as anglophone Africa has been doing.

The metaphor of the African state as a political refugee continues with the reality of institutional collapse, psychic bewilderment, and human dislocation. Just as individual refugees need humane intervention and sanctuary, so the African state in places like Rwanda, Liberia, Somalia, Angola, or Burundi must either be rescued by international action or be destroyed by the forces bearing down on them.

An individual refugee needs moral space within which to recover his or her sense of balance. A failed state also needs moral space within which to recover its sense of purpose. An individual refugee sometimes tries to survive by devouring rivals on the run—refugee "eating" refugee, the cannibalism of the dispossessed. The failed state tries to survive by silencing dissent among its own citizens—the rage of the castrated.

Individual refugees can cross borders and seek asylum in other lands. If the failed state is replaced by a government created by the rebel army, it is theoretically possible for the failed state to also go into exile. For example, now that the Rwanda Patriotic Front (RPF) has formed the government of Rwanda, the failed state may seek political asylum in Burundi and become Rwanda's Hutu government-in-exile in Zaire. If the remnants of Rwanda's Hutu-state were granted institutional asylum as a government-in-exile next door, the state would be a literal refugee, not merely a metaphorical one.

But what is involved in this process of state failure in the first place? What is the historical significance, as well as the political meaning, of what we have been observing from Monrovia to Maputo, from Kigali to Kismayu? What does it all mean?

BIRTH PANGS OR DEATH PAIN?

Let me begin with an overarching issue. We used to think that decolonization consisted of the nationalist struggle against colonialism, the final granting of independence, and the replacement of national flags and national anthems. Colonially educated members of the African elite like Joseph Ki-Zerbo and Ali Mazrui came to the fore, and some of them, like

Kwame Nkrumah and Léopold Sédar Senghor, took the reins from the colonial masters and ruled the colonial state. The question that has arisen recently is whether real decolonization is not winning formal independence but the collapse of the colonial state itself. It is not changing the guard, raising the new flag, and singing the new national anthem while leaving the old structures intact. Rather, it is the cruel and bloody disintegration of colonial structures. Decolonization should no longer be equated with political liberation.

Have Somalia, Rwanda, Liberia, Angola, and Burundi been experiencing the death pangs of a dying order? Or are we witnessing the real but devastating birth pangs of a genuine postcolonial order? Are the refugees victims of the horrors of their dying order or are they brutalized witnesses to a rebirth? Whatever the case, we need to understand what constitutes state failure, as opposed to what represents political collapse.

THE STATE IN SIX FUNCTIONS

Before we can assess if and when the state has failed, we need to clarify its basic functions. Six state functions seem to be particularly crucial. First, sovereign control over territory; second, sovereign oversight and supervision (though not necessarily ownership) of the nation's resources; third, effective and rational revenue extraction from people, goods, and services; fourth, capacity to build and maintain an adequate national infrastructure (roads, postal services, telephone system, railways, and the like); fifth, capacity to render social services such as sanitation, education, housing, fire brigades, hospitals and clinics, and immunization facilities; and sixth, capacity for governance and maintenance of law and order. In looking at the process of state failure, we should not limit ourselves to the sixth function. We may get earlier notice of a state in decay if we work out indicators of performance in all six areas. The African state may show signs of desperation long before it has been reduced to a political refugee.

Clearly the government of Angola lost sovereign control over a large proportion of the country's territory, with consequences for control of resources, infrastructure, revenue, social services, and governance. Many people have been displaced.

As to sovereign oversight over the nation's resources, very few African states have control in this area. Mining companies, oil companies, distant controllers of coffee and cocoa prices, and rampant local corruption have all drastically diluted the concept of resource sovereignty in Africa. Long before the African state failed to govern, it failed to control its resources.[2] (Sovereignty over resources is not to be confused with ownership of resources, which may be in private hands.) In South Africa political apartheid may be dead, but economic apartheid is still alive and well.[3] Most of the best land, the best jobs, and the mineral wealth are owned by whites, local or foreign.

Does state failure begin in resource impotence? Did the Zairean state fail because of its impotence in overseeing the country's immense resources? Is the Zairean state trying to be rescued? Is the Zairean state already a political refugee?

The tax system is also in a shambles in one African country after another. A state that cannot collect revenue from citizens, goods, and services is a state heading for ever-deepening decay. It is also a state on the lookout for handouts from foreign donors.

The state also has a role in building and maintaining an infrastructure and providing essential social services. A state that lags farther and farther behind in providing roads, sanitation, education, postal services, and so on is headed for massive popular discontent and either regime failure or state collapse.

A state's failure to perform the sixth function—governance and maintenance of law and order—sometimes precedes collapse. Clouds of death and displacement appear, and both the people and the state are on the verge of seeking political asylum.

At this stage the state is no longer able either to monopolize the legitimate use of violence or to set rules as to when the citizens may legitimately use violence.

But in reality a state succeeds or fails in relation to wider societal configurations as well. In postcolonial Africa ethnicity continues to be a major determinant in a state's success or failure.[4] Yet here too Mother Africa presents its contradictions. The road to state collapse or state displacement could be either having too many groups in the process or, paradoxically, too few.

Previous failures of the state in Uganda were partly due to the very ethnic richness of the society—the striking diversity of Bantu, Nilotic, Sudanic, and other groups, all of which were internally diverse. The political system was not yet ready to sustain the immense pressures of competing ethno-cultural claims. Lives were lost, and thousands were displaced. Similarly, Ethiopia under Mengistu Haile-Mariam also drifted toward state failure, partly because the system was unable to accommodate its rich cultural and ethnic diversity. Mengistu's tyranny did not foster free negotiations, compromise, or coalition-building among ethnic groups. Again, lives were lost and thousands were displaced.

But how can a state fail or collapse because it has too *few* ethnic groups? At first glance it looks as if Somalia is such a case.

George Bernard Shaw used to say that the British and the Americans were two peoples divided by the same language. It may be truer and more poignant to say that the Somali are a people divided by the same culture. The culture legitimizes the clans, which are among the central causes of discord. The culture also legitimizes a macho response to interclan stalemates and thus interclan feuds.

Interclan rivalries among the Somali would decline if they were confronting the competition of other ethnic groups within some kind of plural society. The Somali themselves would close ranks if they were facing the rivalry of the Amhara and the Tigre in a new plural society. Thus major schisms can develop even in a culturally homogeneous society.

In any case, Somalia could be studied as a plural society comprising many clans rather than many "tribes." The single culture of the Somali people may be a misleading indicator, because the pluralism of Somalia is at the level of subethnicity rather than ethnicity. That disguised pluralism of Somalia was exploited by Siad Barre to play off one clan against another. Siad Barre's tyranny, which lasted from 1969 to 1991, turned out to be the high road to the destruction of the Somali state. The Somali became more than nomads; they also became refugees.

The real contrast to the plural society as a threat to the state is the *dual* society. The plural society endangers the state by having more sociological diversity than the political process can accommodate. Paradoxically, the dual society endangers the state by having too little sociological differentiation for the politics of compromise. This category—the dual society—is understudied and even unrecognized.

THE DUAL SOCIETY AND POLITICAL TENSION

As we grapple with new levels of conflict in Africa, from Kigali to Kismayu, from Maputo to Monrovia, we ought to at least try to identify which sociopolitical situations are particularly conflict generating.

A good deal of work has been done already on the plural society in Africa—societies like Nigeria, Kenya, and Tanzania, which have many ethnic groups and political allegiances. What has yet to be explored adequately is the phenomenon of the dual society—a country that is fundamentally divided between two groups or two geographical areas. The state in a dual society has different vulnerabilities from the state in a plural society. In a dual society two ethnic groups may account for well over three-quarters of the population.

Rwanda and Burundi are such dual societies. So is Sudan. But they are dual societies in very different senses. Rwanda is an ethnically dual society whose fatal cleavage is between the majority Hutu and the minority Tutsi. Burundi is similarly bifurcated between these two groups.

Sudan is a regionally dual society, divided between a more Arabized northern Sudan and a Christian-led southern Sudan, but it is ethnically plural. Internally both northern and southern Sudan are culturally diverse.

Cyprus is both regionally and ethnically dual between Greeks and Turks. There is a stalemate between partition and confederation, which the United Nations has been trying to mediate since the early 1960s. Czechoslovakia was also both ethnically and regionally dual between Czechs and Slovaks; in the postcommunist era, the country has partitioned itself into separate Czech and Slovak republics. In effect, the state of the old Czechoslovakia has collapsed and split in two.[5]

The riskiest situations are not those involving a convergence of ethnic duality and regional (territorial) duality, as in Cyprus or Czechoslovakia. While it is true that a concentration of two ethnic groups in separate regions increases the risk of territorial or political separatism and secession, in human terms that may not be the worst scenario. The riskiest form of duality is that of ethnic differentiation without territorial differentiation. Thus, there is no prospect of a Cyprus stalemate, keeping the ethnic groups separate but peaceful, or a gracious parting of the ways as in Czechoslovakia, creating separate countries. The two groups are so intermingled in neighborhoods, and at times so intermarried, that a soured ethnic relationship is an explosive relationship.

Rwanda and Burundi fall precisely into this category. The two groups are intermingled within villages and even within streets. Rwanda also happens to be the most densely populated country on the African continent, estimated in the 1980s at 210 persons per square kilometer (about 540 persons per square mile).

In close quarters ethnic duality without regional separation can be a prescription for deep-seated hate. Rwanda's and Burundi's tragedies are a combination of ethnic duality, population density, geographic intermingling, and the legacies of colonial and precolonial relationships.

Northern Ireland is another case of ethnic or ethnoreligious duality— Protestant and Catholic—with considerable intermingling in the north.

There is no possibility of partitioning the north into a Catholic sector to be united with the Irish Republic and a Protestant sector loyal to the United Kingdom. A second Irish partition is not in the cards, not least because the population of the north is too geographically intermingled. Inter-communal hate is therefore immediate and at close range.

Is Sri Lanka in the Indian Ocean also a dual society, with the two biggest groups being the majority Sinhalese and the minority Tamils? The population is intermingled to a substantial extent, but the Tamil Tigers rebel group is fighting for a separate Tamil homeland in predominantly Tamil areas. Militarily the country faces a stalemate at the moment.

Ethnically dual societies are vulnerable to polarization. The absence of potential mediating coalitions through other groups makes the Rwandas and Burundis of this world more vulnerable than ever to periodic ethnic convulsions. Cultural frontiers without territorial frontiers and a dual identity within a single country can create a society at war with itself.

Sudan is also a country at war with itself, but its duality is regional, not ethnic. Both northern and southern Sudan are multiethnic, but the south is culturally more indigenous, less Islamized, and led in the main by Sudanese Christians. The first round of the civil war between the two regions occurred from 1955 to 1972, ending with the Addis Ababa Accords of 1972.[6] In 1983 a second round of the Sudanese civil war broke out, and it has raged ever since. Both civil wars created hundreds of thousands of refugees and internally displaced persons. The first round of the civil war (1955–72) was more clearly secessionist. The southern rebels wanted to pull out of Sudan and form a separate country (a precursor of the Czechoslovakia solution). The second round of the Sudanese civil war has been more ambivalent about secession. Indeed, southern military leader Colonel John Garang has emphasized that he stands for democratization of all of Sudan rather than for southern secession.

There is some nationwide intermingling between southerners and northerners, but on a modest scale. The real divide is region-specific and can be territorialized, unlike the division between the Hutu and the Tutsi in Rwanda.

The speed of killing in Rwanda in April and May 1994 was much faster than almost anything witnessed in the Sudanese civil war—some two hundred thousand people were killed in Rwanda within a two-week period. "There are no devils left in Hell," declared the cover of a May 1994 issue of the American newsmagazine *Time*. "They are all in Rwanda."[7] More people were killed later, and a third of the country's population was subsequently displaced or dislocated.

Of course, the state has not collapsed in Khartoum, even though it has no control over parts of the south. Second, unlike the Rwandan national army, the Khartoum national army has not been seeking out helpless civilians for slaughter, from refugee camps to hospitals. However, over the long run both civil wars have been very costly in human lives and human suffering. Sudan has yet to find a solution to its violent dualism. Its split cultural personality between north and south has so far been more divisive than its split ethnic personality among diverse tribes and clans.

The dual society continues to cast its shadow over plural Africa—from Zimbabwe (Shona versus Ndebele) to Algeria (Arab versus Berber), from Nigeria (north versus south) to the tensions of Kigali and Khartoum.

While Czechoslovakia was a case of both ethnic and territorial dualism (Czech versus Slovak), and Burundi and Rwanda are cases of ethnic dualism (Tutsi versus Hutu) without territorial dualism, Yemen is a case of territorial dualism (north versus south) without significant ethnic dualism. Is the distinction between the self-styled Republic of Somaliland and the rest of Somalia a case of territorial dualism without ethnic dualism, as in the case of Yemen? Or is there subethnic dualism between the two parts of Somalia that make it more like the case of Cyprus (Greek-Cypriot versus Turkish-Cypriot), both ethnically distinct and territorially differentiated? Alternatively, the two parts of Somalia may represent an *intermediate* category of dualism, equally prone to internecine conflict. Displacement is less of a problem in the Republic of Somaliland than in the rest of Somalia.

The United Republic of Tanzania is a more artificial case of dualism between the much smaller member, Zanzibar, and the mainland of the old Tanganyika. Arab refugees from the 1960s are beginning to return to Zanzibar. There have been heated political disputes between the two parts of the United Republic, with separatist sentiments sometimes manifested on the island of Zanzibar and sometimes, paradoxically, also manifested among mainlanders. Is it a situation to which the present secretary-general of the OAU (himself a Tanzanian) should pay special attention? Are there ominous ethnoreligious warning signs in Tanzania that we ought to monitor?

IN SEARCH OF NATIONAL SOLUTIONS

Every African government has continued to walk that tightrope between too much government and too little government. At some stage an excess of government becomes tyranny; at some other stage too little government becomes anarchy. Either trend can lead to a failed state. Anarchy produces more displacement and more refugees than tyranny, yet it is easier to get political asylum if one is a victim of tyranny than if one is a victim of anarchy.

A basic dilemma concerning too much government versus too little hinges on the party system. There is little doubt that one-party states tend toward too much government. This has been the case in most of Africa. On the other hand, multiparty systems in Africa have often degenerated into ethnic or sectarian rivalries resulting in too little control. This tendency was illustrated by Ghana under Hilla Limann, Nigeria under Al-Hajji Shehu Shagari, and the Sudan under Sadiq el-Mahdi in the 1980s. The state was losing control in all three cases.

Uganda is feeling its way toward one solution to the dilemma: a no-party state. Concerned that a multiparty system would only lead to a reactivation of Uganda's ethnic and sectarian rivalries, President Yoweri Museveni lent the weight of his name, office, and prestige to the principle of a Uganda without political parties for at least five years. A major challenge would be how to prevent a no-party system from becoming a one-party system.

There are other solutions to the dilemma between multiparty anarchy and one-party tyranny. One possibility is a no-party presidency and a multiparty parliament. This arrangement could give a country a strong executive with extensive constitutional powers, but one who is elected in a contest between individuals and not between party candidates. Parliament or the legislature, on the other hand, could remain multiparty. The president would not be allowed to belong to any political party. A system of a presidency without a political party may indeed give undue advantage to Africa's millionaires (e.g., black Ross Perots or other M.K.O. Abiolas), but that may be the price of a no-party presidency in a multiparty society.

Both Uganda and Ethiopia may be drifting away from a strict unitary state. Federalism, which used to be a dirty word in most of Africa outside Nigeria, is gaining new legitimacy. Nigeria has a lot to teach Africa about federalism—both good lessons and bad.

Another major unresolved dilemma lies in civil-military relations. Although military rule often leads to too much government, civilian rule in countries like Nigeria and Sudan has sometimes meant too little government. Politicians squabble among themselves and sometimes plunder the nation's resources. If military regimes have too much power and civilian regimes have too little control, coup-prone countries like Nigeria and Sudan have to find solutions for the future or face the prospects of destruction and displacement.

In 1972, Dr. Nnamdi Azikiwe, the first president of Nigeria after independence, proposed a constitutional sharing of power between the military and civilians. It was called *diarchy*, a kind of dual sovereignty. Dr. Azikiwe was roundly denounced, especially by intellectuals and academics who were against military rule. But the dilemma has persisted in Dr. Azikiwe's own country, Nigeria, and elsewhere in Africa: What mechanism can be used to bridge the gap between the ethic of representative government and the power of the military?

What would dual sovereignty look like? Africa has experienced other forms of dual sovereignty before. For example, during the colonial period Sudan was supposed to be an Anglo-Egyptian condominium, the dual sovereign being the King of Egypt and the monarch of Great Britain exercising jurisdiction over the Sudanese. However, since Egypt was occupied by the British from 1872 on, the Anglo-Egyptian condominium was more Anglo than Egyptian.

Has Egypt evolved an internal diarchy since the revolution of 1952? Has Azikiwe's dream found fulfillment in Egypt, however imperfectly? Or is the Egyptian system still in the process of becoming a diarchy? Starting as a military-led system in 1952, it has certainly become increasingly civilianized, but it still falls short of full power sharing.

But does Africa have such a model of dual sovereignty involving full power sharing between the military and civilians? Precolonial Africa had all kinds of criss-crossing institution-building. Indeed, in many precolonial African societies, it was not possible to distinguish between military and civilian. There were no standing armies. Warriors were fighters in one season and cultivators in another.[8] But now we have standing armies composed of full-time paid soldiers. And yet they are tempted to be rulers, governors, and policymakers. One method of power sharing is random alternation between elections and military coups, which is more or less what has been happening so far in Nigeria.

An alternative method in coup-prone countries like Nigeria, Burkina Faso, Zaire, and Ghana is the institutionalization of the dual sovereign. Different constitutional arrangements are feasible. One possible constitutional outline could encompass some version of the following.

A whole new concept of a bicameral legislature would come into being: The "civic house" would consist of civilian legislators democratically elected and the "service house" would consist of representatives of the security services (army, navy, air force, and police and prisons). A bill would have to be passed by both houses to become law. The two houses would therefore have to establish legislative negotiating committees to reach compromises acceptable to both. In the United States the House of Representatives and the Senate have special conferences to hammer out compromises on legislation. The civic house and the service house would undertake a similar process.

But in a federal country like Nigeria, would a third house representing the states be needed? The answer is not necessarily. One alternative is to have two-thirds of the civic house consist of members elected on the basis of single-member constituencies and the remaining third consist of representatives of states in the federation.

With regard to the presidency, a system could demand that the running mate of every civilian candidate be a military man or woman. In an election every civilian presidential candidate would have to negotiate with a credible military running mate. Channels of communication would have to be worked out between aspiring politicians and aspiring members of the security forces. Coup-prone African countries would benefit most from such arrangements.

If the civilian president died in office, would his or her military vice-president automatically become president? The answer would vary from country to country. It would not be wise to encourage assassinations of civilian presidents to facilitate succession by their military deputies.

In an election the presidential candidate should always be drawn from the ranks of civilians. The executive branch would therefore have a civilian bias, but the legislative branch would be coequal. The other edge of civilian advantage would be in the *judiciary*. All seven justices of the supreme court would be civilians. But the court would also be advised on every case by three military assessors. The justices would take the views of the three assessors into account, but they would not be bound by these opinions. The tradition of assessors has a long history in British colonial judicial practice.

This system of dual sovereignty should be tried out in coup-prone countries in the first forty years of the twenty-first century. Steps should then be taken to establish a more thoroughgoing civilian democracy. The ultimate goal should always be undiluted civilian supremacy in a viable democratic order.

IN SEARCH OF PAN-AFRICAN SOLUTIONS

It is one of Africa's glories that in spite of artificial borders that have split ethnic groups, there have been very few border clashes or military confrontations between African countries. But one of the tragedies of the African state is that there has not been enough tension and conflict between states. The balance between external conflict and internal conflict has tilted too far to the side of the internal. And as history has shown time and time again, civil wars often leave deeper scars, and are often more indiscriminate and ruthless than interstate conflicts, short of either a world war or a nuclear war. The United States, for example, lost more people in its own civil war than in any other war in its two-hundred-year history, including Vietnam and the two world wars.

Moreover, the history of the nation-state in Europe reveals its persistent tendency to externalize conflict, thus promoting greater unity at home. Each European country developed a sense of nationhood partly through rivalry and occasional conflict with its neighbors. And the consolidation of the European state as a sovereign state was also partly forged in the fire of inter-European conflicts. The Peace of Westphalia of 1648, often credited with launching the nation-state system, was signed after thirty years of inter-European conflicts.

Thus the state system that Africa inherited from Europe was originally nurtured in the bosom of conflict and war. It can even be argued that just as one cannot make an omelet without breaking eggs, one cannot build and strengthen statehood and nationhood without the stimulus of conflict. The only question is whether the conflict is with outsiders or with the state's own citizens. Postcolonial Africa is disproportionately burdened with internalized conflict—which, at least in the short run, is detrimental to both the consolidation of statehood and the promotion of a shared sense of nationhood in the population.

What options does Africa have to change the balance away from civil wars? Clearly, starting interstate wars for the sake of national integration is unthinkable. Even Rwanda and Burundi cannot be encouraged to go to war against each other as an alternative to Hutu and Tutsi civil wars in each. Wars between Rwanda and Burundi are more likely to exacerbate brutality between Hutus and Tutsis than to unite the two states internally. For the foreseeable future the Hutu and Tutsi are condemned to having periodic interethnic conflicts rather than interstate wars, although every ethnic conflagration in one poses a risk of igniting another next door.

In the circumstances, one solution to a civil war is to take sides. State borders are entirely artificial, and the rules of the game are basically external rules of conventional international practice. Should Africa be entirely governed by these rules or can other moral rules be equally compelling in certain circumstances?

One factor to consider is which side in a civil war is the side of the majority. Another factor is which side in a civil war is likely to save more lives. In the 1994 civil war in Rwanda the government side represented the majority Hutu in the country. On the other hand, the Tutsi-led RPF was a more disciplined military force and seemed likely to be more concerned about saving lives.

In the absence of external conflicts confronting African states, one casualty might well be, as we indicated, neutrality in a civil war. In the face of carnage and anarchy outsiders might well have to take sides in civil conflicts. International partisanship is bound to play havoc with the interests of the refugees, but refugees are pawns in power struggles in any case.

In May 1994 the choice in Rwanda was between the rudiments of the Hutu state (ethnically majoritarian but recklessly destructive) and the RPF (led by the minority Tutsi but significantly more disciplined and seemingly capable even of self-criticism).[9] The RPF seemed to be the only credible alternative to the systematic genocide that the Hutu state appeared to be carrying out.

Almost all African countries are unstable to some extent, but we must not assume that they are unstable for the same reasons. Conflict prevention requires greater and greater sophistication in diagnosing conflict-prone situations. Unfortunately Africa is full of contradictions—conflict generated by too much government versus conflict generated by too little; conflict generated by too many ethnic groups, as distinct from conflict ignited by too few ethnic groups. These contradictions complicate diagnosing Africa's problems.

What is the solution in acute state failure or political collapse? Before total collapse the state may be the equivalent of a political refugee—desperate, bewildered, sometimes destructive, but fundamentally moaning to be rescued from a nightmare that may in part be of its own making.

One option is restoration of order through unilateral intervention by a single neighboring power. When Tanzania invaded Uganda in 1979, troops marched all the way to Kampala. Tanzania then put Uganda under virtual military occupation for a couple of years. The Ugandan state was temporarily a refugee camp. Tanzania's intervention was very similar to Vietnam's intervention in Cambodia to overthrow Pol Pot, except that the Vietnamese stayed on in Cambodia much longer. The question arises as to whether Yoweri Museveni's Uganda should have intervened in Rwanda in April 1994 the way Julius Nyerere's Tanzania intervened in Uganda fifteen years earlier.

Another intervention scenario is that by a single power but with the blessing of a regional organization. Although there is no African precedent, there is an Arab example: Syria intervened in the Lebanese civil war with the blessing of the League of Arab States, and the Lebanese state was a refugee camp with Syria as a sentry.

A third intervention is inter-African colonization and annexation. In a sense this is a kind of self-colonization. One precedent is Tanganyika's annexation of Zanzibar in 1964, which resulted in part from pressure by U.S. President Lyndon B. Johnson and Sir Alec Douglas-Home of Great Britain. The West wanted to avert the danger of a Marxist Cuba on the clove island off the East African coast. Nyerere was persuaded that an unstable or subversive Zanzibar would be a threat to the mainland. He got the dictator of Zanzibar at the time, Abeid Karume, to agree to a treaty of union, very much like the British used to convince African chiefs to accept "treaties" by which they ceased to be sovereign. No referendum was held in Zanzibar to see if the people wanted to cease being an independent nation. The annexation of Zanzibar was the most daring case of what became, de facto, Pax Tanzaniana.

The fourth solution to political collapse is regional integration, in which the state as a political refugee is integrated with its host country. In the longer run, one solution to Rwanda and Burundi may well be a federation with Tanzania. Hutus and Tutsis would no longer maintain their own ethnic armies, and those soldiers would be retrained as part of the federal army of the United Republic of Tanzania. German colonialism before World War I had leaned toward treating Tanganyika and Rwanda-Urundi as a single jurisdiction.

In the short run, joining Rwanda and Burundi with Tanzania would be safer than union with Zaire in spite of the shared Belgian connection with Zaire and the link with the French language. Tanzania is a less vulnerable society than Zaire and a safer haven for Hutus and Tutsis. It is significant that Hutus and Tutsis on the run are more likely to flee to Tanzania than to Zaire in spite of ethnic ties across the border with Zaire. Moreover, Hutus and Tutsis are becoming partially Swahilized and should be able to get on well with "fellow" Tanzanian citizens. As citizens they would be assimilated in due course; their former refugee state would be integrated.

A fifth scenario for conflict resolution is an African security council, complete with permanent members in the style of the United Nations Security Council. The permanent members could be Egypt from North Africa, Nigeria from West Africa, Ethiopia from eastern Africa, and the Republic of South Africa from southern Africa. All four pivotal states are chosen partly by reason of their population size. Nigeria and South Africa also have considerable material resources. Egypt, Nigeria, and South Africa are also countries of wider influence. If the four countries survive, they are bound to be major political actors in the twenty-first century. There should also be three to five nonpermanent members. The principle of permanent members would be reviewed every thirty years. For example, in thirty years it may be necessary to add Zaire as a permanent member to represent central Africa. In times of crisis should this council meet at the level of African heads of state? Should each permanent member have a veto or not? These issues would have to be addressed.

The sixth scenario for conflict resolution in times of political collapse is the establishment of a pan-African emergency force to put out fires from one collapsed state or civil war to another and teach Africans the art of a Pax Africana. Should this pan-African emergency force be independently recruited and trained in a specialized manner, or should it be drawn from units of the armed forces of member states? And how will training, maintenance, and deployment be funded? Certainly the successes and failures of the ECOWAS Monitoring Group (ECOMOG) in Liberia should be studied carefully in preparation for this new venture. Renegade states are sometimes basically refugee states. Brutal villains in power are also pathetic casualties of history, so the emergency force should be trained to use minimum violence.

Another scenario is a high commissioner for refugees and displaced Africans under the OAU. Africa has the biggest concentration of displaced persons in the world, so Africans should start to assume responsibility for at least some of the functions of refugee relief. What is demanded is not merely Africa's participation in refugee relief, but its leadership. An OAU high commissioner for refugees and displaced Africans, equipped with the resources to coordinate with the UN High Commissioner for Refugees (UNHCR), would be a start.

The eighth scenario of conflict management would entail ad hoc solutions from crisis to crisis, using mediation and searching for solutions rather than using force. Such ad hoc efforts are definitely better than nothing and could constitute a major part of Africa's search for a peace established and maintained by Africans themselves.

The OAU's Mechanism on Conflict Prevention, Management, and Resolution is in the more modest tradition of intervention. For the first time the continental intergovernmental organization has an active role in internal civil conflicts. Modest as the mechanism is, it signifies a qualitative shift in the orientation of African heads of state.

RETREAT FROM THE STATE?: A CONCLUSION

On the other hand, are there signs that parts of Africa are in retreat from the state? The collapse of colonial institutions in places like Rwanda and Somalia has been both a short-term catastrophe and a long-term opportunity. The catastrophe lies in the obvious human suffering and large-scale loss of human life. The opportunity is for creating genuine supracolonial alternatives including a retreat from the state as a mode of political organization.

Within these supracolonial alternatives in turn there are other subscenarios. One is to attempt some kind of re-traditionalization, a partial revival of forms of governance more in keeping with Africa's cultural past. The Republic of Somaliland (a breakaway fragment of Somalia before the 1990s) has attempted to recreate the traditions of governance through clan consensus (*clanocracy*), which was more characteristic of Somali political culture before European colonial rule. If this kind of retraditionalization survives, or if it is extended to the rest of Somalia as a basis for ordered anarchy, it would constitute a partial retreat from the state.

The Republic of Sudan is retraditionalizing by attempting a policy of Islamization and Arabization. The political and legal cultures are getting Islamized, and in the 1990s universities have been replacing the English language with Arabic. Sudan is therefore another illustration of decolonizing by a "revivalist" strategy. Sudan is not attempting to retreat from the state; it is only trying to Islamize the state.

As we indicated earlier, the government of Yoweri Museveni in Uganda is aspiring to create a no-party state—a kind of postmodernist solution to the ravages of postcoloniality. In the past Uganda has suffered from ethnic factionalism arising out of multiparty disarray (the pull towards anarchy). She has watched her neighbors experience the dictates of single-party systems (the pull towards tyranny). President Museveni is seeking a political order that would ensure popular participation without political parties—a quest for democracy without tribalism. Museveni is in retreat not from the state but from the party-state.

Ethiopia after Mengistu Haile-Mariam is indeed in partial retreat from the state. The new constitution of Ethiopia attempts to decentralize power to the ethnocultural regions. At least in legal theory, the system is designed to evolve into a confederation of cultures, with each ethnocultural region enjoying considerable control over its resources as well as its way of life. If this experiment succeeds, Ethiopia may remain a set of boundaries on the map, but be a diluted state in reality.

What all this means is that Africa is experiencing a high-risk rebellion not only against the colonial state but sometimes against the state per se as a mode of governance. Many African societies are ill at ease with the state as a system of governance; most are bewildered about what to do about it. But in a few places an agonizing reappraisal of the state and the beginnings of a retreat from it have begun.

Places like Hong Kong may have become post-state phenomena. Places like Somaliland and Ethiopia may be retreating towards a pre-state utopia, as the twentieth century brings its colonial curtain down.

But behind the scenarios and the search for solutions, behind the pain and the anguish, is the paramount question: Are we facing birth pangs or death pangs in the present African crisis? Are we witnessing the real bloody forces of decolonization as the colonial structures decay or collapse? Is the colonial slate being washed clean with the blood of victims, villains, and martyrs? Are the refugees victims of a dying order or are they traumatized witnesses to an epoch-making rebirth? Or is the future of the state itself in Africa at stake?

Is this blood from the womb of history giving painful birth to a new order? How much of it will be order without the state? In the past Africa combined statehood with statelessness. Are we on our way back to that equilibrium?

> The blood of experience meanders on
> In the vast expanse of the valley of time
> The new is come and the old is gone
> And time abides a changing clime.

3

THE AFRICAN ROLE IN CONFLICT MANAGEMENT AND RESOLUTION

B. A. Kiplagat

INTRODUCTION

To most outside observers who are unfamiliar with the intricacies of local life in various African countries, the crises that erupt in Africa seem unexpected and unpredictable. But those who look for telling signs and signals know that these crises could have been anticipated and predicted.

The eruption in Rwanda shocked the world. People wondered how such an explosion could occur without warning signs. But in 1993 I was part of a fact-finding mission to Rwanda to determine how the Arusha accord was holding and to assess the humanitarian needs in Rwanda. When I arrived in Kigali, it was immediately evident that the country was in crisis. The two-year civil war had created great hardship. I visited a refugee camp with more than one hundred thousand residents, who were living under appalling conditions. The total number of displaced persons approached 1 million. The continuing war, the displaced persons, and all the political currents put the government under siege. The implementation of the Arusha accord, which was viewed by outsiders as the basis for peace and reconciliation, was at a standstill. Those who signed it did not do so with any commitment or conviction. It appeared that power-sharing would not work, that elections could not be held, and that the war would continue. Moreover, weapons were being stockpiled in villages for the horrible events that unfolded in April 1994.

Rwanda's minister of foreign affairs visited Kenya in 1985. His purpose was to convey a message to Kenyan President Daniel Arap Moi regarding Rwandan refugees in Uganda, Kenya, and Tanzania, most of whom had been out of Rwanda for twenty-five years. He indicated that Rwanda was not in a position to receive these refugees back, since Rwanda was one of the most densely populated countries in the world. He asked that the countries where the refugees were residing accept them on a permanent basis. But the desire of these refugees to return to Rwanda became one of the principal motives behind the founding and mobilization of the RPF. Alarm bells should have been ringing throughout the region in 1985, but the matter was dismissed and the situation confronting Rwandan refugees remained unchanged.

How is it that the international community did not realize the magnitude of the social and political problems facing the people of Rwanda? Is it because the country is landlocked and only infrequently visited by journalists, business people, and diplomats? Or do we not want to confront crisis situations until they force themselves on us?

Although the start of the Rwandan civil war caught the international community by surprise, regional powers took early steps to try to bring the parties to the bargaining table. Tanzania convened peace talks in Arusha and after a year of negotiations the Arusha accord was signed. In this case negotiations were organized without waiting for the political/military situation to ripen. But that is unusual. In most crises in Africa, negotiations are delayed and neighboring powers and the broader international community are slow to respond. This is what happened in Sudan. Despite the fact that many international NGOs were deeply involved in relief work in Sudan, the war went on for four years before external initiatives were taken to promote peace negotiations. In 1984 church NGOs called a meeting to discuss what role they might play in promoting peace in Sudan, but since they had no funds and little peacemaking experience, they were reluctant to get involved. Similarly, in Mozambique the war went on for many years before the Kenyan government took initiatives in 1988 to promote a dialogue between the antagonists.

Nairobi is the headquarters for a large number of NGOs that operate throughout Africa. Many of them are trying to promote peace, and they are very active in relation to Sudan and Somalia. But they show no interest in Djibouti, Sierra Leone, Senegal, Zaire, or Uganda. People can kill one another for years without their neighbors, Africa-wide organizations, or the international community raising an alarm. Attention is focused on these crisis spots only after the media, particularly television, project the suffering into living rooms around the world. Once international attention is focused on an African crisis, the prospective mediators and conflict resolvers compete with each other to get a piece of the action. This was the case with Mozambique, until Sant'Egidio finally took the lead. Even then countries continued to jostle for position, trying to obtain places as observers at the negotiation table, to become peace monitors, or to train the future unified Mozambique army. But after the Mozambique peace agreement was signed, interest in the international community waned and so little support was given to implementation of the agreement that it almost came unstuck.

EARLY WARNING AND PREVENTIVE DIPLOMACY

One way to deal comprehensively with Africa's conflicts is to compile and update an inventory of trouble spots. This inventory should include cases where conflict is still at nascent stages and should identify organizations and governments that have taken peacemaking initiatives in particular conflicts.

It is critical to identify indicators of incipient conflict. One such indicator is the refusal of a country to permit refugees to return home. Rwanda and Burundi are examples. The government of Rwanda was not prepared to welcome back its own citizens scattered in the East African region, despite the relative peace and stability then prevailing in Rwanda. Hutu refugees from Burundi living in Tanzania and Zaire did not trust the Bagaza regime sufficiently to risk returning to Burundi. These were unrecognized and unheeded signs of actual or impending crisis. The most dramatic sign of crisis was the Rwandan government's appeal in 1985 for host countries to absorb Rwandan refugees permanently.

Another indicator of trouble is large numbers of citizens fleeing a state, particularly when those fleeing are prominent leaders, like intellectuals and politicians. Movement of exiles out of a country is a sign that oppression is growing, and it lays the basis for a rebel movement to develop outside the country. Leaders who flee into exile often have strong constituencies remaining at home, often based on regional, clan, and tribal structures. These leaders are able to mobilize political support from their exile bases.

Growth in the numbers of displaced persons is another sign of trouble. The numbers of displaced persons in countries like Rwanda, Somalia, and Liberia have grown enormously in recent years. When these displacements come to the attention of the media, the world becomes aware of the conflict. But many other cases of serious dislocations have not been recognized by the outside world. Even though such countries may project images of stability to the outside world, all is not well and catastrophes could develop.

Other indicators of impending trouble are significant growth in security budgets, changes in the structure of the security forces, and increases in personnel recruited into such branches of the security forces as the police, paramilitary organizations, and the secret service. These changes may indicate that the political leadership is losing its grip and resorting to the security apparatus to control the population. Excessive reliance on this apparatus often causes further weakening of the political system.

When so-called "security zones" are declared out of bounds for foreigners, generally the government is trying to hide something. In such cases outside observers should ascertain whether a major security operation is under way and whether human rights are being violated.

When an African regime recruits lobbyists to burnish its tarnished image in western capitals, particularly in Washington, observers should be alert to trouble. This occurs with increasing frequency and is a sign that the bad publicity a country is receiving can be altered only by professional image makers.

A significant increase in the size of prison populations, especially the numbers of political and quasi-political prisoners, is another sign of political trouble, repression, and increased likelihood of impending crisis. Changes in prison populations usually reflect arbitrary arrests, harassment, and imprisonment of political opponents.

These indicators can be used as social-political barometers of the level of actual or potential conflict in African countries. They can also provide a rough index of when diplomatic intervention should be initiated to head off full-fledged conflict. Countries that show signs of turmoil are prime candidates for preventive action of one kind or another by neighboring states and the international community.

When the international community begins to ask questions about signs of trouble, local officials usually dismiss the inquiries with explanations that what has been witnessed is simply the work of agitators and that the troubles will soon be resolved. The international community generally accepts these bland reassurances and rarely presses further. If there is an outbreak of violence in a remote part of the country, the authorities generally pass off the problem as the work of bandits or disgruntled elements. For many years Mozambique's government referred to the Mozambique National Resistance (RENAMO) as disorganized bandits supported and financed by the "white racist regime" of South Africa. But it does not really matter who is supporting a dissident group when a full-fledged conflict is under way.

The task of peacemakers is to grasp the nettle with both hands and deal with the problem in its early stages. Otherwise, it will fester and spread, not only to other parts of the country but to surrounding countries as well. Neighbors should be the first to get involved, and if their efforts do not succeed, then other countries or organizations outside the region could be encouraged to take the initiative. The precise character of the most appropriate intervention cannot be predetermined; it will depend on the nature and seriousness of the conflict, the local and regional actors involved, and the readiness of those intervening to become engaged. The peace broker must fully commit himself or herself to launch a peace initiative and to sustain the commitment. Regardless of whether this party eventually becomes a principal negotiator, the party needs to remain engaged.

POLITICAL AND INSTITUTIONAL CONDITIONS OF PEACE

A successful peace process requires attention not only to reaching a peace accord but also to fashioning a new political structure and a constitution that will support long-term peace. There is too little debate and discussion in Africa about the nature of the state. During the period of single-party or military states, political debate was declared subversive, and some leaders strongly advised civic organizations to keep away from politics. Africa is now paying the price for not confronting these political issues. Innovative and responsive structures could have prevented the conflict Africa is now experiencing. It is urgent that Africans undertake a full discussion of alternative political structures, to enlarge and deepen the political process and to protect human rights.

New political structures must share certain basic principles, such as the separation of powers. But new political structures must also be responsive to local realities, particularly the ethnic composition of the society and its culture and history. These structures will take different forms depending on the country, but fundamental rights for individuals and communities must be enshrined in all constitutions. Laws from an earlier period that restricted free association, freedom of expression, and registration of voluntary organizations and permitted political detention must be eliminated in the new democracies.

The basic principles of democracy must be observed. Some Africans argue that the principles of human rights and democracy apply only to the western world. And a few western governments are beginning to concede that some democratic principles should be sacrificed in Africa as a means of reducing ethnic conflict. Doubts are even being expressed about whether democracy can actually function in Africa.

But democracy has an honored history in Africa. Even in precolonial African societies, basic human rights were observed and democratic procedures were established for the selection and removal of leaders. If a leader violated his oath of office by being unjust, cruel, or dictatorial, the council of elders, who had the right to remove a leader from office, would meet and decide what to do. In the majority of such traditional societies, decisions were arrived at through consensus. Stable societies were built on the rule of law.

The primary causes of the present instability in Africa are violations of human rights and the maladministration of justice. More attention must be given to Africa's judicial systems, because a stable state cannot be achieved without a strong, impartial, and well-administered system. Judicial systems are often undermined by those in power, and decisions are often dictated. The strong arm of the government can easily manipulate poorly paid civil servants. Lawyers who demonstrate independent thought are often not promoted to the bench. Judges and civil servants in the judicial system often seek government loans for money to invest or to meet essential financial obligations, but approval of a loan usually requires support from a senior government official and this process compromises judicial independence. Judges are sometimes subjected to blackmail as well. Renewal of contracts for foreign judges usually depends more on how cooperative they have been with the executive branch than on the wisdom of their judicial opinions.

The rule of law is the cornerstone of conflict prevention. In addition to helping strengthen judicial systems, the international community must stand firm in its insistence on democracy, fundamental human rights, and the rule of law in African countries. Countries can legitimately make some adaptations to their social, cultural, and religious environment, but basic human rights must be protected. All countries need to be moving toward just, participatory, and democratic forms of government.

Freedom of speech and expression are among the basic democratic principles to be protected. Freedom of the press is particularly important.

Control of radio broadcasts has been a powerful weapon in the hands of dictatorial governments. It has been used to promulgate government ideologies and to strengthen government control. The former government in Rwanda made devastatingly effective use of the radio in unleashing the 1994 massacres. Control of the radio can be an instrument of either peace or war, so its governance needs to be carefully considered. The state should not have a monopoly on control of the radio, and radio should not be used to undermine democracy, individual freedom, or human rights.

Too many African countries are controlled by strong executives who demand absolute loyalty from civil servants. The fact that civil servants cannot exercise independent judgment is a major source of instability and conflict. Even constructive criticism is considered disloyal. Survival and advancement are dependent on supporting and implementing the regime's policies. Such an environment breeds inefficiency, corruption, and even sabotage. An independent civil service, on the other hand, can be a major resource for economic and social development and for conflict prevention.

AFRICAN CONFLICT MANAGEMENT AND RESOLUTION EFFORTS

How can Africa's conflict be successfully managed or resolved? Cases of success are not numerous. An early example is the temporary resolution of the Sudanese civil war in the Addis Ababa agreement of 1972, which was brokered by Emperor Haile Selassie of Ethiopia, the World Council of Churches, and the All-Africa Conference of Churches (AACC). Sudan enjoyed a period of relative peace and stability for eight years after that agreement, but its abrogation by the Khartoum government led to a resumption of the war. The 1991 peace agreement in Angola generated great hope, but these hopes were soon shattered. The Nairobi agreement, reached in 1985 with the help of the Kenyan government to end fighting in Uganda, was never implemented, since Yoweri Museveni opted for a military solution. The Rome Accord, reached in 1992 and facilitated by Sant'Egidio with help from Kenya and Zimbabwe to end the Mozambique war, has been largely implemented.

The Liberian case is a tragic one. The parties involved went through all the necessary motions and signed an agreement providing for a UN monitoring force, but the conflict continues and there is no sign that it will end soon. The problem of the Tuareg, which affects a number of Sahelian countries, has never been completely resolved. The Djibouti situation is like a dormant volcano, despite recent elections. It would be useful to study these and other examples of efforts to resolve internal, postindependence conflict in African states. Why have so many efforts failed and so many agreements come unstuck? Conclusions from such a study could help guide future efforts at conflict resolution.

What is the current African capacity to promote conflict resolution? Not many institutions have experience. Some examples can be cited, such as the AACC in relation to Sudan and elsewhere, ECOWAS in relation to Liberia, the Kenya government in relation to Uganda and Mozambique, the Tanzania government in relation to Rwanda and Burundi, and Inter-Africa Group in relation to Somalia. The small number of experienced individuals and institutions derives from the low priority that this problem has been accorded both by Africans and by the international community. But this situation is changing. Conflict resolution is now close to the top of the agenda for many organizations.

AACC has been active in sending peace missions to Zaire, Angola, Burundi, and Rwanda. It is currently coordinating the work of five NGOs trying to keep the IGADD-managed Sudan peace initiative on track. But AACC is overwhelmed by the magnitude of the problem and the demands being placed on it. The unit within AACC responsible for conflict resolution is very weak in both personnel and financial resources. AACC leadership has an enlightened approach to peacemaking and AACC has a strong network throughout the continent. AACC can also call on the worldwide church for support. Its experience and institutional memory from earlier activity in this sphere give it a strong base on which to build. It will inevitably become a leader in this field and in doing so will fulfill the prophetic call of the founders of AACC in 1958 when they stated in the Ibadan Declaration, "The continent of Africa will face unparalleled events during the remaining decades of this century—welcomed by some and rejected by others. We hope the church will be a comforter, reconciliator, and counsel with the support of our brothers and sisters abroad."

In 1994 IGADD, consisting of six countries of the Greater Horn, widened its mandate and took on the mammoth task of trying to bring peace to Sudan. Despite enormous administrative problems, lack of resources, and suspicion among the parties in conflict, IGADD made a good start. The commitment of the region's leaders to bring peace to Sudan should be encouraged and supported.

The OAU is also taking important steps forward. Although a conflict resolution unit has been established within OAU, old habits and bureaucratic procedures die hard. Some member states are still clinging to the principle of noninterference in the internal affairs of other countries. To wait for a request for intervention from the country itself would in many cases permit serious violence and mass killings to continue. Moreover, OAU member states sap the potential of the organization through cynicism about the OAU's lack of capacity and power, a cynicism that destroys the organization's self-confidence. We must recapture the vision of a handful of men who, at the sixth Pan African Conference, held in Manchester, England, in 1946, made a commitment to liberate the whole of Africa by the end of the century. With the accession to power of the African National Congress (ANC) in South Africa in 1994 their vision has been fulfilled. We now need a new vision and a major effort to resolve the conflicts ravaging the African continent.

The OAU deserves special attention and support, because it is a potentially formidable force. The OAU needs to be open to ideas and energy emanating from new organizations in Africa, including African NGOs and subregional international organizations. These organizations will also benefit from the vision and purpose of the OAU, and both can benefit from cooperative efforts to mobilize the resources needed to bring peace to Africa.

Another important organization is the African Academy of Sciences (AAS), which has organized a working group to address Africa's internal conflicts. Its first set of publications has already been produced; the insights suggest that the organization has much to offer in the effort to understand and resolve Africa's conflicts.

Organizations and governments outside Africa are also demonstrating concern and taking initiative. Over the past thirty years outside organizations have provided relief assistance in war situations. But the problems persist. The most notable example of external intervention came in December 1992 when the American government spearheaded an international intervention on a massive and unprecedented scale in Somalia.

Those of us in the region had watched helplessly as the Somali state disintegrated, causing a mass exodus of Somalis pouring across the borders, seeking refuge in neighboring countries. The situation deteriorated rapidly; there was no time for the neighbors to consult or consider what might be done. When the UN Security Council endorsed the American initiative, we gave a sigh of relief, hoping that the worst part of the pending disaster had been averted. But as the days and weeks passed, a complex political picture began to emerge. The American time perspective was unrealistically short and the sudden obsession with the arrest of Mohamed Farah Aideed was misguided. The plan began to unravel, further complicated by misunderstandings between UN headquarters in New York and UN staff in the field, as well as between American forces and those from other countries.

A major mistake was the failure of the Americans to consult broadly, particularly with Somalis and neighboring states. Unfortunately, leaders of the countries of the Greater Horn were preoccupied with their own problems. Uganda was concerned about Rwanda, Kenya was undergoing major political changes, and Ethiopia was trying to manage its own political transition. But consultations would have helped, because there was a strong negative reaction from key Somalis, both internally and among those exiled abroad, and the neighboring states had different ideas than the Americans about how to proceed. The whole intervention was undertaken in haste, and it is not really surprising that it did not achieve what it was expected to. Food did reach the people, but at enormous cost, and instability within the country increased. What is required is an integrated and comprehensive strategy that would encompass work at the grass roots, setting up local administrative councils, disarmament, demining, demobilization, and efforts to get the clan leaders to cooperate in solving the nation's problems.

One very unfortunate consequence of the intervention in Somalia is that the death of American soldiers and anti-American demonstrations in Mogadishu may cause the United States to refuse to intervene again in Africa. As it grapples with internal conflicts, Africa needs the support of the international community, particularly that of the United States.

Several steps must be taken to improve the chances of conflict resolution in Africa. First, efforts need to be made to raise the awareness of political leaders and opinion makers both in Africa and abroad to ensure clearer and more compassionate understanding of what conflict resolution requires. Second, an inventory and classification of conflicts needs to be prepared. Such a survey should include a detailed profile of the causes and character of each conflict, as well as organizations and individuals engaged in peacemaking. Another inventory should list African organizations that might be called on, along with indications of their strengths and weaknesses. Third, when an initiative is taken like that of IGADD in Sudan, the effort needs to be focused and sustained. It is a long process requiring great effort, and financial support will probably be required from the international community. Fourth, more attention must be given to the successful implementation of peace agreements. Outside parties involved in the negotiations often lose interest when implementation begins, particularly when they encounter problems. Adequate resources and sustained support are required for successful implementation.

As we tackle conflict resolution in Africa, let us work cooperatively, linking our expertise and resources toward a common goal. Successful conflict resolution requires major efforts both at the grass roots and at leadership levels. Only a multidimensional approach will advance the process of helping Africa through these difficult times and enable it to emerge as a strong, stable, developing continent, able to make its own contribution to world peace and stability.

4

THE U.S. ROLE IN MANAGING AFRICAN CONFLICTS

Lessons from the Past

Donald Rothchild

In the post–Cold War period, U.S. policymakers, concerned with promoting a stable international order in which democratic regimes and economic trade and investment can be nurtured, have found themselves with little choice but to become involved in internal conflicts in Africa.[1] As the sole remaining great power (in military terms, at least), the United States cannot stand aside, as the rather belated and limited response to the 1994 Rwanda crisis showed, while destructive conflict jeopardizes effective governance.

U.S. involvement in facilitating a resolution of Africa's contemporary conflicts has taken many forms: conflict prevention (information gathering, measures of reconciliation, and pressure for human rights and democratization); behind-the-scenes support for dispute mediation by African third-party actors (Nigeria in Sudan, Zaire in Angola); backing a regional actor (ECOWAS in Liberia, OAU in Rwanda); assisting an extra-continental actor (Britain in Zimbabwe, Portugal in negotiating Angola's internal settlement, Italy in the Mozambican negotiations); promoting an international organization's initiative (UN in Congo, Somalia, Rwanda, Liberia,

Namibia, and Angola after the signing of the Bicesse accords); pressure on local actors to negotiate (South Africa, Sudan); humanitarian intervention and diplomatic facilitation (Somalia); organization of a regime transition (Ethiopia); and direct third-party mediation between internal parties (Sudan 1989–92, Zaire 1992) as well as between international parties (the Angola government, South Africa, and Cuba regarding a settlement in Angola and Namibia).

What lessons have we learned from recent American efforts to promote peace in Africa? In examining the American role in peacemaking, I will try to establish two general propositions: first, that the United States will tend increasingly to conduct its peacemaking initiatives indirectly, under the auspices of the UN, OAU, or other official and unofficial actors; and second, that U.S. diplomats should view implementation (or post-agreement peace building) as linked to the prenegotiation and negotiation processes. In setting forth the latter proposition, I will also point to a number of ways that peace accords can be crafted to promote an ongoing negotiation process that may lead to a sustained democratic outcome.

THE UNITED STATES AS FACILITATOR OF AFRICAN PEACE ACCORDS

The necessity for international negotiations and mediation efforts arises from the failure of global and regional collective security mechanisms and the decline of domestic norms of conflict resolution. When the weak state lacks the capacity to regulate society effectively, and relations between ethnic and nationality groups become irregular and possibly belligerent, an imbalance between conflict and stability develops, sometimes, as in Rwanda, with terrifying consequences. One option, adopted by a majority of state elites, is to attempt to eliminate the opposition or to force its capitulation (for example, Uganda (1966 and 1987), Burundi (1972), Nigeria (1966–70), and Rwanda (1994)).[2] Because such an option is straightforward and involves no shift in preferences, it is often preferred by those in power. Another option, which often occurs after a "mutually hurting stalemate" has been reached, is to seek to reestablish a balance between conflict and stability by negotiating with subnational interests, as in Zaire (1965), Sudan (1972), Zimbabwe (1979), Angola-Namibia (1988), and South Africa (1994).

The difficulty of mediating internal insurgencies becomes even more pronounced when guerrilla movements have an ethnic or nationality dimension—the main but not the exclusive focus of this chapter. No doubt, this reflects the high level of emotion surrounding such encounters and the great reluctance of state authorities to deal with the leaders of guerrilla movements. State leaders fear that such diplomatic contacts may give these movements a measure of international respectability, even legitimacy.[3] Consequently, the general prospects of mediating Africa's civil wars seem limited. Nevertheless, under certain circumstances—such as the emergence of identifiable bargaining parties, a mutually hurting stalemate, leaders intent on a political solution, external pressures to reach agreement, and a mediator actively on the scene—third-party intervenors have sometimes been successful.

The status and power of third-party actors are crucial. Various African leaders, singly or jointly, have undertaken mediatory initiatives in African state-substate conflicts. Emperor Haile Selassie proved an effective arbiter during the 1972 Sudanese peace negotiations and, in the changed circumstances of the post–Cold War period, a six-state ECOMOG force has had some success in stabilizing the situation in Liberia. Other African leaders have wielded less control over political resources and therefore proved less successful. Although they have displayed considerable skill in bringing rival parties to the bargaining table and then hammering out a logical plan of action, they were constrained from the outset by the unwillingness of the negotiating parties to shift their preferences and perceptions to the extent necessary to make the agreement stick. A great power such as the United States has a distinct advantage in such situations. Because it can exert significant pressures and offer meaningful incentives, it is in a position to push hesitant elites to make a commitment.

In terms of different kinds of conflict situations, third-party peacemaking initiatives taken by U.S. diplomats in Africa can be divided into five basic types: pressures on internal actors to negotiate, indirect mediatory activity, direct mediation, military-diplomatic intervention, and the implementation of agreements.

1. *Pressure on internal actors to negotiate.* Diplomats and legal scholars are increasingly inclined to accept as doctrine the right of states to intervene in the domestic affairs of other states to pursue humanitarian objectives and advance the peace process. It is therefore not surprising that a powerful international actor such as the United States will intercede in various state-subnational conflicts that violate the rights of certain groups of citizens and thus pose a serious threat to the stability and well-being of the world community. In doing so, the United States has aligned itself with various state (Ethiopia under Haile Selassie) or insurgent (National Union

for the Total Independence of Angola (UNITA)) leaders, with very real consequences in the resulting levels of conflict.

The United States has protested, sometimes in an unpublicized manner, abusive actions directed at ethnic minority peoples. In addition to general U.S. concerns for human rights and the protection of the international system from grave instability, the United States has in the past used its influence to intervene in various internal conflicts. Examples of such actions include the closure of an American embassy (Amin regime in Uganda), the temporary cessation of bilateral aid projects (Uganda), termination of programs by such U.S. government agencies as the Export-Import Bank or the Overseas Private Investment Corporation (Uganda, Rhodesia, South Africa), and economic sanctions (South Africa, Rhodesia, Uganda).

More recently, the U.S. Senate took a strong stand on human rights violations in Sudan, forcefully criticizing the Sudanese government for engaging in a campaign of "ethnic cleansing" against the Nuba people in Kordofan Province and opposing the extension of further World Bank or International Monetary Fund (IMF) loans while this situation persists.[4] In September 1993, the United States and the European Union urged an end to the Kenya regime's practices of ethnic cleansing in the Rift Valley, linking the cessation of such human rights violations to any discussions on the resumption of multilateral economic assistance.[5] Subsequently, however, these U.S. and European Union pressures gave way to a more pragmatic approach: At the Paris Club meeting in December 1994 the western donors agreed to meet Kenya's $800 million external financing needs. Nevertheless, to the extent that these statements of principle uphold international norms of behavior, they may represent a contribution to policies and practice.

2. *Indirect mediatory activity.* In this context, indirect mediatory activity refers to U.S. backing for a formal mediatory effort mounted under the auspices of another party. This approach can involve U.S. support for a private, informal mediator (as in former President Jimmy Carter's attempts to mediate between the Ethiopian government and the Eritrean People's Liberation Front [EPLF] in 1989) or for a formal third-party undertaking led by another state or by a regional or international organization. The line between indirect mediatory activity and direct mediation is sometimes quite blurred. In Somalia following the U.S. humanitarian intervention in 1992–93, for example, American diplomats mediated certain local conflicts on their own. However, in the critical negotiations of March 1993, where the fifteen factional leaders agreed in Addis Ababa to set up a Transitional National Council, UN and Ethiopian government leaders played a

prominent third-party role, facilitated by a behind-the-scenes American diplomatic effort.

There are numerous instances of indirect mediatory action by the United States under the auspices of other state actors. In the case of Rhodesia (Zimbabwe), where Britain was still recognized the world over as the colonial power, U.S. diplomats appropriately played a supporting role during the critical Lancaster House peace negotiations in 1979. Although Britain's foreign secretary, Lord Peter Carrington, exercised a firm hand during the conference sessions, not everything proceeded according to plan, making American intercession critical at one key juncture. When the future constitutional arrangements were being discussed, it became necessary for U.S. diplomats, who had been observing the procedures closely, to come to the support of the British mediators. They offered financial grants to an independent Zimbabwe for such broad purposes as agriculture and education. This American initiative proved very timely, for it enabled the Patriotic Front negotiators to save face and the conferees to avoid a breakdown over the land issue.

U.S. indirect mediatory activity was present in Angola as Zaire and, subsequently, Portugal attempted to mediate between the two internal adversaries—the Popular Movement for the Liberation of Angola (MPLA) government and the UNITA insurgents.[6] The first such peacemaking effort was undertaken by Zaire's President Mobutu Sese Seko, with the backing of a number of governments in the region as well as the support of the Soviet Union and the United States. Mobutu organized an African summit initiative at his residence in Gbadolite in June 1989, which resulted in a reluctant handshake between the adversaries as well as an agreement in principle on a cease-fire and moves to promote national integration. Given the hasty way in which the agreement was hammered out and the vagueness of the principles, it was not surprising that the accord proved extremely hard to implement. A series of mini-summits attempted to thrash out the differences over the reintegration of the civil service and armed forces. U.S. policymakers did not put enough pressure on UNITA leader Jonas Savimbi to change his preferences, and it was not long before the civil war resumed.

Portugal, with encouragement from Angolan President José Eduardo dos Santos, then accepted the call for a new third-party initiative. In 1990–91, Portuguese officials chaired a series of talks between representatives of the Angolan government and UNITA. This time the two great powers actively supported the Portuguese mediators, in contrast with their earlier lack of urgency over the Gbadolite initiative. The great powers jointly sponsored a meeting in Washington, D.C., attended by the Angolan government, UNITA, and the Portuguese. This meeting produced the so-called Washington Concepts Paper, a conceptual framework for the Portuguese-mediated talks. The Washington agreement on basic negotiating principles gave new impetus to the flagging deliberations at Bicesse, Portugal. With U.S. and Soviet observers in attendance at the subsequent rounds of discussions, the negotiators reached a compromise on such knotty issues as the formation of a national army, setting dates for the cease-fire, the timing of multiparty elections, and the international monitoring process. Not only did the great powers play an important role in pushing the parties to sign the interim cease-fire accord, but they also took part in the Joint Political-Military Commission that oversaw the transition process.

The Bicesse accords proved difficult to implement, because UNITA leader Savimbi refused to accept the outcome of the 1992 elections held under this agreement. Fierce encounters ensued, as UNITA overran some 70 percent of the country in 1993, followed by a powerful counterattack by a heavily rearmed and externally advised Angolan army late in the year. Against a backdrop of sharp military encounters, heavy casualties, and destroyed cities, the ongoing UN-mediated peace initiative in Lusaka, assisted prominently by U.S. special envoy Paul Hare and various regional diplomats, carefully worked out the Lusaka Protocol of November 1994. With government forces increasingly dominant and regional and international pressures on Savimbi increasing, the insurgent leader shifted from a bid for military victory to a willingness to negotiate what amounted to the continuance of the Bicesse accords, with minor modifications. In reaffirming the Bicesse process, the Lusaka Protocol set out details for a cease-fire, a second round of presidential elections, demilitarization, disarmament, and the formation of a unified army and national police force. To be sure, the protocol represents a fragile peace arrangement. But the UN has deployed 7,000 observers to oversee the implementation process and the confidence-building measures embodied in the agreement may allay some of Savimbi's fears, so there is reason to hope that the protocol can form the basis for a return to normalcy in Angola.

Indirect mediatory action by the United States was also important during the critical phase of the 1992 Mozambican negotiations between the government and RENAMO. These talks were jointly mediated by the Italian government, the Roman Catholic Archbishop of Beira, and the

Catholic lay organization Sant'Egidio. In its capacity as an official observer, the United States sent legal and military experts to Rome to help iron out the details; these experts consulted with the contending parties on a regular basis about the cease-fire and military-related issues. In addition, the United States agreed to participate in the UN-supervised effort to implement the peace agreement.

In sum, the United States has been reasonably effective in promoting its larger peacemaking objectives, especially when acting behind the scenes to support middle-range powers or regional and global organizations. Combining the political legitimacy of international organizations and other official and nonofficial actors with the financial and strategic capabilities of a great power such as the United States puts the resulting coalition of mediators in a strong position to influence the preferences of disputing parties.

3. *Direct mediation.* U.S. third-party mediation of African conflicts can involve either unofficial or official actors, or a combination of the two. The combination of individual and state initiatives was illustrated by former President Jimmy Carter's efforts to promote a dialogue between the Ethiopians and Eritreans in 1989, which was followed by U.S. authorities' direct involvement in mediating between the main Ethiopian adversaries. In October 1990 and February 1991, Assistant Secretary of State Herman Cohen held talks in Washington with Ethiopian government and EPLF delegations, but he was unable to narrow the differences. Then, as the insurgent Ethiopian People's Revolutionary Democratic Front (EPRDF) forces approached the perimeters of Addis Ababa and President Mengistu Haile-Mariam fled the country, the United States interjected itself into the unfolding crisis. At the request of the caretaker government and the opposition movements in the field (the EPRDF, the EPLF, and the Oromo Liberation Front), Cohen convened a meeting in London on May 27 and facilitated a relatively smooth transition to the new EPRDF regime.

Official and nonofficial American mediators also intervened actively at various points in the Sudanese civil war, both to protect the distribution of relief supplies and to facilitate the peace process. In 1989, U.S. pressures on the Sudanese government to allow various public and private aid agencies to deliver food to the rebel-controlled areas in the south were largely successful. These successes led to calls to negotiate an end to the war itself. Assistant Secretary Cohen met separately with Dr. John Garang, chairman of the Sudan People's Liberation Movement (SPLM) and commander-in-chief of the Sudan People's Liberation Army (SPLA), and Prime Minister Sayed Sadiq el-Mahdi. Shortly afterward, former President Jimmy Carter laid plans for a new peacemaking exploration. Although this meeting was delayed by General Omer al Bashir's military coup, Carter did manage to bring representatives of the al Bashir government and the SPLM-SPLA together in Nairobi in late December 1989 for an unsuccessful encounter.[7]

Further American peace initiatives followed. In March 1990, Cohen undertook a new peace effort, involving a cease-fire and disengagement of forces, the establishment of a monitoring force, and the convening of a national constitutional conference. Proposals on disengagement were followed by counterproposals, with little agreement about who was to occupy the vacated area. The process of peacemaking gradually stalled, in part because Sudanese military authorities were suspicious of intrigues between the SPLA and the Americans. Variants of the 1990 proposals, including federalism, military disengagement, and multiparty democracy, were subsequently presented by Cohen and other nonofficial intermediaries, to no avail.[8] The United States had little success in negotiating a Sudanese peace accord between the government and the insurgents by means of a direct approach, and U.S. diplomats appeared to turn to indirect mediatory activity. Subsequently, the United States gave quiet backing to the Nigerian-mediated Abuja peace process in 1992–93.

The greatest success in direct U.S. mediation in recent years involved the international negotiations on Angola and Namibia, which led to a settlement among sovereign states, not internal parties. Even so, the Angola-Namibia accords do show that U.S. initiatives can sometimes result in settlements of Third World conflicts that endure over time.

From independence in November 1975 to the signing of the Angola-Namibia agreements in December 1988, the conflict among the Angolan nationalist movements (UNITA, MPLA, and, until the early 1980s, the National Front for the Liberation of Angola [FNLA]) was a civil war exacerbated by the ties that these nationalist movements had to various external powers. The MPLA government was bolstered by Soviet military equipment and Cuban combat troops while FNLA, and for a time UNITA, received Chinese military equipment following decolonization, U.S. military assistance around independence and after 1985, and South African military assistance and combat units during all phases of the war.

As the civil war continued into the 1980s, and the MPLA and UNITA forces, backed by their external allies, became locked into a costly stalemate, the various local and international actors became increasingly responsive to proposals for international—but not internal—negotiations. The inability of UNITA and South African forces to achieve a decisive victory at Cuito

Cuanavale and the Cuban military strike at the Calueque Dam, which demonstrated Cuban air superiority, represented a change in the balance of military power within Angola that raised the costs of further South African offensives.[9] Prospects for a serious peace initiative were also greatly advanced by the mid-1980s change in the great powers' perceptions of one another. With Moscow and Washington shifting from adversarial to cautiously cooperative relations, it was an opportune time for a concerted effort to settle outstanding regional conflicts.[10]

The critical negotiations to end the deadlock and bring about an international settlement gained momentum in late 1987 as the Angolan government accepted the idea of linking a phased withdrawal of Cuban forces from Angola with Namibia's independence. The Angolans and the South Africans were far apart in their thinking on the timetable for Cuban redeployment and withdrawal, aid for the UNITA insurgents, and the terms for South Africa's disengagement from Namibia, but Assistant Secretary of State Chester A. Crocker nonetheless concluded that the moment was ripe for a major third-party peace initiative. What followed was an eight-month effort to overcome the regional deadlock through peaceful means. With Crocker as chair, the representatives of Angola, Cuba, and South Africa met secretly in London to explore the Angolan proposal for a four-year withdrawal of Cuban forces. This May 1988 meeting was followed by sessions in Cairo, New York (twice), Cape Verde, and Brazzaville. Persistent behind-the-scenes Soviet and American communications between these adversaries, and even some pressures on their allies, resulted in the acceptance of general principles on Namibia's independence, a phased Cuban withdrawal, verification, and formal recognition of the U.S. role as mediator. "Momentum," Crocker writes, "helped keep our flock headed in the right direction."[11]

At the Geneva talks that followed, the conferees issued a joint statement announcing a de facto cessation of hostilities and a series of steps, including proposed dates for Namibia's independence and for the withdrawal of Cuban and South African troops from Angola. At successive meetings in Brazzaville in the fall, the parties narrowed the gaps between them on the issue of Cuban troop withdrawal, agreeing that the pullout would take place over a twenty-seven-month period and that two-thirds of these soldiers would leave during the first year while the remainder were redeployed by stages to the north. With these thorny questions behind them, the conferees tackled the remaining points of contention: the verification procedures and the language of the protocol. Although the MPLA government and the various external intervenors remained antagonists, they had nonetheless managed to act pragmatically with respect to the issue of regional peace in southern Africa. But this pragmatism did not carry over to the related task of reconciling the MPLA and UNITA. Only as the great powers came to recognize the urgency of reaching an internal agreement and, under the auspices of a Portuguese mediator, to exert significant influence on their respective allies, did a fragile and largely ineffective peace agreement materialize.

4. *Military-diplomatic intervention.* The Somali humanitarian intervention may be something of an anomaly in terms of an American-sponsored military action. In the Somali case, the Bush administration dispatched a U.S. military force of 25,000 to an African country in 1992–93 to ensure a safe environment for the delivery of relief supplies and to begin the process of national reconciliation.[12] The aberration here lies in the will of U.S. policymakers to intervene in situations where an African state fails. State loss of influence, even breakdown, has also occurred in Rwanda, Liberia, and Sudan, and appears a distinct possibility in Zaire and Sierra Leone. Yet, with the exceptions of Liberia and to some extent Rwanda, the international community seems reluctant to become actively involved in the internal affairs of these countries, in part because citizens in the United States and elsewhere are not anxious to shoulder the burden.

Although Somalia set a precedent in terms of a successful American-led military effort to ensure food deliveries to the starving, there was a question of the mission's ability to disarm the militias and restore order in Mogadishu, to cope with the threat of national disintegration, and to undertake the diplomatic initiative necessary for political healing. In essence, the problems in Somalia, with its clan-based rivalries and ethnoregional antagonisms (i.e., the Isaak rebellion and separatism in northern Somalia) are primarily political in nature.[13] The U.S. military could not be expected to create political legitimacy through the use of force. It could only use the momentary opportunity of its overrule to create the conditions in which diplomacy could take place. It did secure the main transportation routes, pacify a sizable area of the country, and, to a limited extent, disarm the main factional leaders. However, the negotiations that took place under its aegis have proved a tenuous basis for peace.

The diplomatic process that followed the U.S. military intervention represented a cautious effort to contain the most destructive elements of the conflict, in particular seizing some of the weapons controlled by the warlords and thereby forcing them into the political arena. While the American team did mediate some of the local conflicts on their own, such as that between Ali Mahdi and Aideed, the main task of negotiating a national agreement fell to Ethiopian leader Meles Zenawi and the UN, with the Americans playing a supporting role. In March 1993, the fifteen main factional leaders met in Addis Ababa under UN sponsorship. They agreed to establish a Transitional National Council that would include the various clan leaders plus three elected representatives from each of the country's eighteen regions. Subsequent meetings of clan leaders were held in the year that followed, but with inconclusive results. Somalia's clan leaders remain powerful, and the situation on the ground is still highly fluid and uncertain.

5. *Implementation of agreements.* Again, the picture in terms of successful outcomes is mixed. While agreements ending internal wars in Zimbabwe, Mozambique, and Namibia were implemented effectively, those in Ethiopia-Eritrea (1962), Sudan, Angola (1991), and Rwanda collapsed. In Angola (1994) and Liberia the linkages between state and society remain fragile, and it seems premature to rule out a return to civil strife.

For societies such as Angola, which lack a consensus on the rules of the game, the 1991 Bicesse accords inevitably came under severe strain, not only because of a lack of precision about the terms of the agreement itself, but also because of the pressures of intransigent politicians, ethnic and regional claims, and intense struggles for government positions and fiscal resources. The result, all too frequently, has been an undermining of agreements in the early phases of the transition period. Unable to build societal support for the new peace accords, the pressures on the new regimes prove overwhelming.

Particularly where mediators have limited leverage over the rival parties during the postagreement phase, as in Sudan and Angola, the task of facilitating a return to stable relationships has proved daunting. A number of third-party intermediaries have stepped into these conflicts, only to find that they had little space to maneuver when using diplomatic means to change actor preferences and perceptions. In these worst-case scenarios, the mutually hurting stalemate that is supposed to lead to a reevaluation of alternatives came to seem endurable, leading to a contest of wills that often had little to do with rational calculations on maximizing economic interests.

The drive for security, combined with the ambitions and fears of communal leaders, has frequently undermined African peace agreements. Perhaps the most dramatic case of implementation failure leading to disastrous incoherence is that of Angola in 1992. UNITA's leader Jonas Savimbi, fearing a loss of influence and status after his likely defeat in the second runoff election for the presidency, withdrew his military officers and troops from the unified army and renewed the armed struggle. The UN peacekeeping force on the scene was undermanned and underfunded and proved ineffective in monitoring the demobilization and reintegration provisions of the Bicesse accords before the elections. Consequently, the scheduled runoff election never took place, and Angola resumed its civil war.

The Sudanese implementation failure was another tragic breakdown of leadership. Although there were initial indications of a return to normalcy following the signing of the Addis Ababa agreements, it became apparent by the mid-1970s that the government of President Gaafar el-Nimeiri had shifted its position on the question of southern autonomy. Nimeiri intervened in the process of selecting a president for the High Executive Council in an effort to ensure the nomination of his preferred candidate. Other signs of a changed outlook on accommodating the south soon followed. The government proceeded with the building of the Jonglei Canal (despite its alleged drying effects in the swampy Sudd area), altered the electoral processes, proposed border changes between north and south, located the oil refinery in northern territory at Kosti, imposed *Sharia* law on the whole country, and redivided the south into three regions. Outraged by these so-called provocations, southerners resumed the civil war and the carefully crafted Addis Ababa agreement was undermined.[14]

Two other examples of implementation failure—both with highly destructive consequences for civilians and military personnel—involved the collapse of the Ethiopian-Eritrean and Rwandan settlements. In the first case, Emperor Haile Selassie changed the UN-orchestrated agreement on federation between Ethiopia and Eritrea (which had remained in effect from 1952 to 1962) and then reincorporated Eritrea into Ethiopia on a unitary basis. The Eritreans were bitter, and the guerrilla action that followed was the beginning of a thirty-year insurgent struggle for self-determination and independence. In the end, as the government in Addis Ababa was toppled by the simultaneous efforts of various opposition movements, the Eritreans secured their goal of independence, gaining international recognition of their separate statehood following an overwhelming EPLF referendum victory in April 1993.

In the case of Rwanda, the terms of the Arusha accords became the source of grave misgivings among Hutu militants. At Arusha, Tanzanian President Ali Hassan Mwinyi mediated between the largely Hutu government *Forces Armées Rwandaises* (FAR) and the predominantly Tutsi *Front Patriotique Rwandais* (FPR) insurgents. Mwinyi and Belgian Foreign

Minister Willy Claes reportedly pressured the government/FAR to sign the accords, while Museveni used his special position with the insurgents to encourage them to sign. Subsequently, the *Garde Présidentielle* and other troops from the army massacred over 500,000 Tutsi civilians and some Hutu moderates in 1994, bringing about a collapse of the Arusha accords. Although the Clinton administration stood on the sidelines as tensions built up and genocidal violence ensued, it acted more decisively in the later phases of the crisis by supporting the French intervention and, after the killings had ended, by closing the Rwandan Embassy in Washington and freezing Rwandan-held assets in the United States.[15]

CONCLUSION: THE LESSONS OF THE PAST

In terms of the broader peacemaking process discussed thus far, what lessons from past experience might assist negotiators as they seek to hammer out enduring peace accords? How can U.S. diplomats help to craft agreements that secure sustained adherence? Part of the answer certainly lies in Adam Przeworski's notion of "institutionalizing uncertainty." If the contending parties are prepared to subject their interests to competition, then a system of "spontaneous, decentralized, self-interested compliance may work."[16]

Consolidated agreements and the return to regularized intergroup relations represent a learning experience over time. Incoherent relations, marked by the absence of widely shared norms on managing competition and conflict, sometimes remain a fixed part of the political landscape. Under these circumstances, pragmatically motivated peace accords may not produce the conditional concurrence of the major actors so necessary to surmount the deep differences that emerge during the implementation period. As a consequence, the mutually hurting stalemate, for all its costs, comes to seem bearable, and deadlock takes hold.

Transitions from civil war to peace agreements are inherently difficult processes. Agreements were successfully consolidated in Namibia and Zimbabwe but led to failure and a collapse of state-society relations in Angola, Rwanda, and Sudan. To avoid deadlock and incoherence, political leaders must plan in terms of the long-range consequences of their actions. To prevent agreements from unraveling, leaders must recognize the linkages among the prenegotiation, negotiation, and implementation stages. And they must bring an element of empathy to the bargaining table, role-playing in terms of the concerns of their rivals. Such role-playing, combined with skillful external third-party mediation initiatives and the use of confidence-building measures, may enable these leaders to design peace accords that are sensitive to the impelling needs for strong leadership and political fairness to all sides.

In the end, however, enlightened and effective local leadership is indispensable. Party coalitions must remain firmly in place, able to counter the temptations of defection and political flanking. Unless moderate elements can prevail and networks of reciprocity and political exchange relations can gain a firm hold among these elites, the return to normality will prove well-nigh impossible and the society will be trapped in a destructive environment of incoherence. In light of these factors, a few pointers regarding an effective American peacemaking and peace-building role seem worth putting forward.

- Mediation is essential but not necessarily sufficient to overcome perceptions of menace and intense internal conflicts. Therefore, a mixed record on U.S. mediation efforts should be anticipated. U.S. indirect mediatory action played a supportive role in Zimbabwe and in the Mozambican, (internal) Angolan, Liberian, and Rwandan agreements. Its direct mediation in Ethiopia and (the international) Angola-Namibia accords proved largely successful. But the American record (despite the enormous political and economic resources at its command) in Sudan, Zaire, and Kenya attests to the inherent difficulties of such diplomatic initiatives.

  Clearly a great power has considerable potential to alter the preferences of weaker states through various pressures and incentives. Sanctions applied against South Africa and financial side-payments offered to Zimbabwe's nationalist leaders and Mozambique's insurgents have helped to alter choices. Moreover, in the international negotiations on Angola, Crocker was in a position to influence South African thinking on the urgency of reaching an agreement with its regional adversaries. Not only did he move to implement the sanctions legislation, but he bypassed the South African government to support the anti-apartheid groups on the scene. And he pointedly lodged no protest when the number of Cuban troops was increased in 1987.

  Even though American status and power, in cooperation with the Soviet Union, contributed to the settlement of a number of regional disputes left over from the Cold War, the windup of great power confrontations in Africa has changed things. Internal wars are proliferating, while the great power dimension is disappearing. The impact on American diplomacy is likely to be quite significant in the years ahead. Rather than take the lead in dramatic formal negotiations of the Angola type, U.S. officials can be expected to engage increasingly in behind-the-scenes contacts with prominent local actors and to work increasingly under the auspices of regional, continental, and global organizations. Such a team effort will likely be more useful in preventing and dealing with conflicts in the twenty-first century, and it can be expected to contribute to another American objective: building up the capacity of these regional and international organizations "to engage early and effectively."[17]

- Lack of precision and clarity of goals at the earlier stages contributes substantially to the collapse of agreements during the implementation phase. To be sure, a degree of ambiguity may be necessary to gain the adversaries' consent to an accord, but in the long run the price of such ambiguity may prove extremely high in terms of implementing agreements under conditions of political and economic uncertainty. In Liberia, the Cotonou agreement, which left a number of issues to subsequent meetings for reasons of political expediency, did distribute positions on the Transitional Government among representatives of the main parties on a roughly proportional basis. However, the agreement did not set out organizing principles regarding representation in the cabinet. Such vagueness on an important political issue contributed to later misunderstandings. It is not enough to bring about a handshake between adversaries, as was the case at Gbadolite; rather, peace is furthered when the parties have carefully negotiated their differences and genuinely accepted the new rules of encounter. It is unrealistic to expect shortcuts to secure a quick and easy transition from civil war to normal relations.

- In many instances it is advantageous to have a strong, American-backed mediator active in all phases of the peace process. A mediator with muscle can play a critical role in manipulating the actors and the outcomes during the negotiation stage and can also be a decisive factor in the implementation phase, serving on the monitoring teams and using pressures and incentives to secure continued compliance with the terms of the agreement.

- There is a great need for an effective state to preside over the implementation of negotiated agreements or peace accords. So long as it is responsive to the legitimate demands of various interests in the period following the signing of these accords, an authoritative state actor, such as that in South Africa, can play a positive role in mediating between the rival internal parties, provided, of course, that it is not captured by one of the competing social interests. It is the strong state that can afford to facilitate the coalition of moderate elements. In Daniel Brumberg's words, such a state is in a position to "forg[e] implicit pacts between reformists in the state."[18]

- A powerful, enlightened, and competent group or party leadership that is committed to maintaining the peace agreement is inevitably a crucial factor in the return to normal relations. This is no easy assignment. In difficult economic circumstances, where one or more of the rivals are insecure and determined to alter past inequities, African governments must reconcile previously dominant ethnic elements while assuring the general public that constructive change will ensue. Should transformation move too slowly, as may be the case in South Africa, there is always the possibility that party coalitions will become unstable and flanking parties will emerge, championing extremist, parochial interests. In the fluid situation that follows a transition to more democratic forms, group and party leaders must follow a steady course in defending the accord; any lapse on their part is likely to discredit the peace process.

- To prevent the unraveling of agreements, it is important for leaders to emphasize the notion of fairness toward all major interests during the transition period and after. Democracy can be interpreted quite widely here, embracing a number of the measures and principles of governance that inspire confidence in the agreement among political minorities. Prominent among such confidence measures are provisions on power sharing, decentralization, cultural autonomy, respect for traditional authorities, proportional regional allocations, balanced recruitment into the civil service and army, competitive elections systems, and demilitarization. Unless the adversaries can deal with these issues effectively during the negotiation stage, serious conflict will probably emerge during the complex bargaining encounters that will inevitably surface when the accords are put into effect.

- Coordination among global, regional, state, and unofficial actors is crucial in implementing peace agreements and promoting a return to normalcy. The costs of properly demobilizing and reintegrating the armed forces are extremely high, but these actions are critical as confidence-building measures among the war-weary public. Similarly, rebuilding the economic and social infrastructure and resuming of economic activity after a civil war are central tasks in a peace-building environment. Exhausted states cannot accomplish more than a minimum on their own and therefore require substantial financial assistance during the transition period.

- Ethnic and religious confrontations continue to mark the African scene, and the will and the means to deal with these post–Cold War disorders are not always in evidence. The problem of resoluteness is compounded by the inexplicit nature of the guidelines under which UN and regional organizations operate. Post–Cold War multilateral institutions lack the rules and regulations necessary to prepare them before states collapse and to determine how to respond once peacemaking and peacekeeping actions are required. The result, as John Gerald Ruggie observes, is that "[t]he United Nations has entered a domain of military activity— a vaguely defined no-man's-land somewhere between traditional peacekeeping and enforcement—for which it lacks any guiding operational concept."[19] Ruggie goes on to note that UN peacekeeping forces are not designed to engage in military enforcement activities; either the states with major military forces at their disposal will increase the capability of the international community to undertake such assignments in an effective manner, or these organizations will witness a decline in their credibility.

To return to the two general propositions about the American role in peacemaking set out in the introduction of this chapter, I find that both are substantiated by the data examined here. The United States seems likely to become increasingly involved in African peacemaking and, as in the Rhodesian/Zimbabwean, Angolan (1990–91 and 1994), Mozambican, and Rwandan negotiations, can be expected to seek its larger objectives through behind-the-scenes initiatives in conjunction with regional, continental, and global organizations. Moreover, the difficulties experienced with implementing agreements, as in Ethiopia/Eritrea (1962), Sudan, Angola (1992), and Rwanda, are likely to lead to a recognition that the stages of prenegotiation, negotiation, and implementation are interlinked. Unless negotiators can hammer out the terms of agreement with some degree of precision and unless they display sensitivity to the fears of key leaders and their constituents, their painstaking efforts to end internal conflicts may be for naught. It is high time that our concern with the negotiation process be matched with careful attention to the consolidation of agreements.

5

A DIPLOMATIC PERSPECTIVE ON AFRICAN CONFLICT RESOLUTION

Robert B. Oakley

L ooking back at significant U.S. efforts to promote peace and resolve conflict in Africa can usefully inform us today on what approaches offer good prospects for success in various situations, as well as what techniques to avoid. For the purposes of this chapter, "significant United States efforts" are arbitrarily defined as those that have involved sustained presidential and cabinet-level attention as part of a deliberate, systematic commitment of diplomatic and usually other assets for at least several months and have included a complementary, institutionalized international peace process (usually involving the UN) in which the United States has been an active participant. The conflict in question has been a major one, involving large-scale civil and/or cross-border combat, with or without external intervention. It does not include more routine, essentially ad hoc activities by the Department of State and U.S. embassies to resolve lesser local conflicts or violent unrest of a temporary, localized nature, which occurs in a dozen or more African countries during an average year.

To define realistically what role the United States should and could reasonably be expected to play in African conflict resolution, it is essential to understand that the political nature of the world and therefore of perceived

U.S. interest and interests in Africa have changed dramatically with the end of the Cold War. So have the interest and interests of other outside powers. Moreover, so has the nature of African conflict. During the Cold War conflict tended to be less widespread and more ideological; to involve fewer states with many fewer people at risk; and to entail less splintering of state institutions and fewer chaotic, violent outbursts of civil strife. (The Congo was more the exception than the rule.)

The following two examples of significant early U.S. efforts at African conflict resolution during the Cold War period—the Congo (Zaire) and Angola/Namibia—demonstrate a sustained, highest level commitment by the United States to use whatever resources were needed for success—short of outright U.S. military force, which was judged unworkable during the Cold War. One can also see the advantages of laserlike concentration of area expertise on the problem at hand and of the ability of those managing U.S. policy to shift tactics as circumstances changed in order to follow a constant strategy.

After reviewing and analyzing these case studies on U.S. conflict resolution during the Cold War period, this chapter will look very briefly at more recent examples of U.S. conflict resolution in Africa. Conclusions will be offered on what can reasonably be expected from the United States today in the way of effort as well as what seems most likely to offer promise of success.

CONGO: 1960–1964

Background

The first major U.S. effort at African conflict resolution began with the United States as no more than a supporter of the peacekeeping initiative taken by UN Secretary-General Dag Hammarskjöld in July 1960, responding to an appeal for help from the government of the Congo in Leopoldville in reestablishing order. Shortly after independence on July 1, the Congo Army (the *Force Publique*, later the *Armée Nationale Congolaise* [ANC]) began to loot and generally disobey orders and threaten the large number of Belgians living in the country. Belgian forces were deployed on July 13 to protect their fellow citizens. The result was an even more violent anti-Belgian reaction and an appeal by President Joseph Kasavubu and Prime Minister Patrice Lumumba to the UN. Violence was so rampant that on July 14 the UN Security Council approved the secretary-general's proposal for a UN peacekeeping force of 10,000 to help restore order, provide humanitarian assistance, and assist (i.e., restrain and retrain) the ANC. The first UN units arrived in the Congo on July 15 and all 10,000 were in place by July 20. The forces eventually reached a strength of 17,000–18,000. The United States provided much of the airlift and logistics, and the USSR also helped transport those within its political orbit (e.g., Ghana). The troops from the United Nations Operation in the Congo (ONUC) came from a number of African states plus Sweden and Ireland. Under Secretary-General Ralph Bunche was the UN special representative in overall command.

Internal Congolese tribal and political divisions soon evolved into a series of armed conflicts, and several regions seceded temporarily, the most important of which was the mineral-rich Katanga province, led by Moise Tshombe. Lumumba benefited from political sympathy and support from the USSR and African socialist states, particularly Ghana, the Sudan, Guinea, and Egypt (the Casablanca bloc). Tshombe had powerful Belgian support, including money, arms, and mercenaries. These internal struggles combined with the ANC's total lack of discipline obliged ONUC to play an increasingly active, direct role in putting down local clashes and trying to end secession and civil war. At the same time ONUC tried to remain neutral in the Congolese power struggle and respond to the nominal authority of President Kasavubu, while adhering to the Security Council's mandate. The United States, European countries other than Belgium, and moderate African states (the Monrovia bloc) supported Kasavubu and ONUC.

As the strife continued with no resolution in sight, Soviet and radical African support for Lumumba became more pronounced. The USSR decided to use the Congo, particularly the secession of Katanga and its obvious Belgian backing (without strong ONUC opposition), as a rationale for an intensive political attack on the United States, the West in general, and the secretary-general. The Soviets charged them with supporting the de facto continuation of colonialism and pro-Western puppet regimes in Africa. The United States made the Congo a top priority after President Kennedy assumed office in January 1961. It became a major test of power between the United States and the USSR, along with Cuba, Indochina, Berlin, and so on. The United States took a more active role and on several issues was at variance with the secretary-general (e.g., the United States wanted more vigorous action against Lumumba, more UN restraint in dealing with Katanga secession, and more forceful disarming of the ANC).

In September 1960 Kasavubu and Lumumba each announced that he had fired the other. Shortly thereafter, ANC Chief of Staff Mobutu Sese Seko assumed power, over time aligning himself with but actually dominating Kasavubu, although the latter was officially reinstated and nominally recognized as president. On December 2, 1960, Lumumba was arrested by Mobutu's ANC and imprisoned near Leopoldville until January 17, 1961, when he was flown to Katanga and killed in prison.

In May 1961 a "government of national unity" was formed, headed by Cyrille Adoula, and gained international recognition. ONUC, Adoula, and Mobutu, with strong support from the United States and despite opposition from the Soviets and their African supporters, gradually made progress in restoring order and putting down rebellion, except in Katanga. Finally, in September 1962 the United States and the UN brought Tshombe to meet Adoula, while ONUC aggressively fought its way into key Katanga locations (to the fury of Belgium and the irritation of the United States). In January 1963 Tshombe formally declared Katanga to be part of the Congo. However, Adoula was unable to maintain control and by mid-1964 a new round of insurgencies broke out, the ANC collapsed, and Tshombe was named prime minister with Belgian support. At the same time, the UN Security Council decided to end ONUC. Unable to control the country, Tshombe stepped down and Mobutu took over in 1965, with U.S. assistance. He has remained in power ever since, most of the time with U.S., Belgian, and/or French support.

Analysis

The United States was successful in achieving its objectives of stabilizing the exceedingly difficult and volatile Congo situation, beating back the serious threat of the Soviet bloc in the Congo, Africa, and the UN, and seeing a friendly government assume control over the country. It did so by virtue of persistence, the expenditure of substantial political capital with western European and African states, the provision of financial support for ONUC, and by either actively supporting or going along with the position of Secretary-General Hammarskjöld and Under Secretary-General Bunche on major issues. The differences in view were not pushed to the breaking point by either party, and the United States regularly voted for the secretary-general's recommendations in the Security Council. By paying close attention to the ever-changing political situation on the ground and cooperating closely, the United States and the UN were able to contain numerous difficulties and prevent them from exploding into major confrontations or conflicts that could easily have put an end to ONUC or brought about a much less favorable outcome. The United States also made good use of its covert assets, notably by enlisting the cooperation and enhancing the power first of Adoula and then of Mobutu.

From the UN perspective, as Brian Urquhart puts it in his biography of Ralph Bunche, "In the Congo Bunche had to defend and maintain in action the basic principle of UN peacekeeping—maintaining peace without using force or taking sides."[1] On occasion, he employed a liberal interpretation of the right of self-defense, and he liberally interpreted the UN Security Council mandate calling for the reintegration of Katanga. In the end, it was a major success for the UN.

Overall, the four-year operation was a success for both the United States and the UN because of continuity of approach and persistent pursuit of the ultimate objective by President Kennedy and Secretary-General Hammarskjöld. They were committed to neutrality within the context of the UN Security Council mandate, they had the political understanding and diplomatic ability to adjust to changing local political situations as well as to withstand external pressures, and they were able to mobilize enough resources to achieve the objectives. These resources included obtaining diplomatic and political support from other governments; deploying and utilizing military forces for ONUC and civilians to administer political and humanitarian matters; and using bilateral U.S. assets, ranging from its leverage over Belgium because of NATO, through CIA action in supporting Adoula and Mobutu, to bilateral economic assistance.

NAMIBIA AND ANGOLA: 1977–1989

Background

The second major U.S. effort at African conflict resolution also involved close cooperation with the UN and Cold War confrontation with the Soviet Union and its allies. The Carter administration took the initiative in pressing for a resolution to the long-standing problem of Namibia, setting up a "contact group" of the five western members of the UN Security Council in 1977 (the United States, the United Kingdom, France, Germany, and Canada) to undertake serious negotiations. U.S. Ambassador to the UN Donald McHenry was the driving force behind the contact group. On September 29, 1978, their efforts produced UN Security Council Resolution 435, calling for the independence of Namibia through free and fair elections; establishing a United Nations Transition Assistance Group (UNTAG); endorsing a special representative of the secretary-general for this purpose; and urging the cooperation of the South African government and the South West Africa People's Organization (SWAPO, a guerilla organization with outside support from African states (Congo, Angola) and the USSR). Intensive negotiations continued until the end of 1980, but to no avail. The South African government was totally intransigent, and SWAPO, which was seen by South Africa as under total communist control, was engaging in superficially positive rhetoric of dubious credibility.

Although the Carter administration made no progress in implementing Resolution 435, it was active and helpful to the United Kingdom in negotiating an agreement on independence for Rhodesia, which had seen substantial black versus white civil war. This was a great embarrassment to Great Britain, which still played a special role by virtue of being the former colonial power. Eventually, the Zimbabwe African People's Union (ZAPU), which was seen as a radical African movement, and its leader, Mugabe, came to power peacefully. This made the South Africans even more fearful of SWAPO, independence, and elections for Namibia.

When the Reagan administration took office in 1981, Assistant Secretary of State Crocker led a thorough review of policy toward southern Africa. The conclusion was that a new direction was needed, both for its intrinsic merit and to make movement on Namibia palatable to South Africa. The Reagan administration decided to link Cuban withdrawal from Angola with the implementation of Resolution 435 on Namibia. Crocker understood the political dynamic of the broader situation in the region, where the USSR and Cuba had been providing massive assistance to the regime (MPLA) in Angola since 1975–76, when they helped beat back a U.S.-backed effort by Zaire, Angolan rebels, and South Africa to overturn the socialist Angolan regime. South Africa, in turn, had since that time been supporting UNITA, the resistance movement to the MPLA, which had a strong tribal base in southern Angola near Namibia. South Africa worked actively with UNITA in opposing SWAPO activities out of southern Angola against Namibia as well as helping UNITA in its efforts against the MPLA inside Angola. The Reagan administration demanded that the Cuban force of 30,000 withdraw, believing that SWAPO would be so weakened and South Africa so reassured that genuine agreement could be reached not only on elections for Namibia but also on a noncommunist post-election political situation that did not threaten South Africa.

The new U.S. strategy produced what Crocker came to call "constructive engagement." South Africa actively discussed and negotiated rather than obstinately refusing to talk and instead relying on the use of military force in Namibia and in support of guerrilla activities against its neighbors

(Mozambique, Botswana, and Zambia as well as Angola) to put down any challenge to its absolute authority. Interestingly, the MPLA, UNITA, and SWAPO were also prepared to negotiate. The United States reinvigorated the contact group, while also closely associating the secretary-general's special representative for Namibia with the new negotiations.

For seven years the United States actively engaged the various parties in negotiations, whose pace and direction ebbed and flowed. Dozens of U.S. bilateral meetings at high levels took place with the South Africans and the MPLA, usually at the ministerial level, some positive and some negative. The contact group was used when deemed advantageous, but most of the work was completed by 1982 on the Namibian side of the linked equation (i.e., clarifying and elaborating Resolution 435 so as to provide explicitly for linkage). The other southern African states (Frontline States) were periodically involved, directly or indirectly, and were kept regularly informed by the United States. There were occasional meetings between the United States and UNITA and SWAPO representatives. There were several combined meetings, the most notable of which was in Lusaka, Zambia, on February 16, 1984, attended by the United States, Zambia (as host), South Africa, and MPLA (Angola).

At that meeting the first agreement was reached pursuant to the U.S. strategy of separating the combatants before seeking agreement on a timetable for withdrawals. (Cuban withdrawal from Angola was to be paralleled by the South African Defense Force [SADF] withdrawal from Angola and then from Namibia, as called for in Resolution 435, so as to ease MPLA fears of being overwhelmed as its Cuban allies departed.) The Lusaka agreement called for Cuban, SWAPO, and SADF withdrawal from a large region of southern Angola adjacent to Namibia. It took a year to implement, but tensions were reduced from 1984 up until a new, major confrontation in mid-1987.

South African suspicions of the United States, the USSR, and the MPLA suddenly surged in 1985, partly due to a successful move by the U.S. Congress to have President Reagan impose economic sanctions on South Africa. It began to take a harder line in negotiations and to build up SADF power for use inside Angola.

One of the "carrots" offered to South Africa by the Reagan administration had been to resist powerful U.S. domestic pressures for sanctions. Thus the imposition of sanctions by Congress made negotiations and mutual trust still more difficult. Nevertheless, the United States (and the UN) put forth more plans and proposals and received partial responses from some parties during 1985 and 1987, but there was no significant diplomatic progress. In the fall of 1987, the USSR instigated an offensive by MPLA forces whose aim was to force the SADF and UNITA back toward Namibia and possibly drive the SADF out of Angola entirely. The MPLA offensive failed and the forces suffered heavy losses as the SADF counter-attacked and occupied or besieged key locations in the south-central region of Angola, most notably the town of Cuito Cuanavale. The United States began actively (and covertly) to support UNITA as a warning to the MPLA and the USSR and as a reassurance to South Africa. Zaire played an important role in supporting UNITA.

This series of actions disrupted the diplomatic as well as the military status quo. It also provided an opportunity for Castro to act militarily to open the way for a Cuban diplomatic initiative similar to that being pursued by the United States. Castro wanted to withdraw to ease the financial and political burdens of indefinite support of such a large force abroad. But he wanted Cuba's withdrawal tied to Namibia's independence and to political agreements that would preserve the MPLA position and stop U.S. and South African military support for UNITA. This could give Cuba an apparent political victory, rather than a military defeat. During the first half of 1988, over 15,000 additional crack Cuban forces plus modern heavy artillery, tanks, and planes were sent to Angola. They fought well, inflicted serious casualties, and forced the SADF to retreat to more defensible positions. This rekindled South Africa's desire for a political settlement rather than continuing the costly war of attrition near or even inside Namibia's borders.

The United States was able to seize the moment to restart talks, including direct talks with Cuba, which were proposed by the MPLA and began in January 1988 in Angola. The Cubans offered a four-year counterproposal to an earlier Crocker timetable for withdrawal. In March 1988 a senior South African delegation came to Washington and agreed to reply to the Cuban-MPLA plan for a four-year Cuban withdrawal. This got the new process under way. By May there were some indications that the USSR was interested in joining the diplomatic game, as the Cubans had already done, to end costly involvement and gain some credit for the solution. This did not occur until later but did contribute to the momentum being generated.

A series of twelve multiparty meetings (United States, South Africa, Cuba, Angola) were held, starting in London on May 2, 1988, then Cairo in June, New York, Cape Verde, Brazzaville, New York again, Geneva, and

Brazzaville again, where agreement was reached on December 13 on a twenty-seven-month withdrawal plan. Further agreements were then completed, and several accords, protocols, and agreements were signed in New York in December 1988, thanks to U.S. mediation. This mediation was specifically endorsed in the agreements, but the United States was not officially a party to it and therefore did not need to seek Senate approval. The final agreement established April 1, 1989, as the date to implement Resolution 435 in Namibia and maintain a cease-fire in Namibia and Angola as withdrawal took place over twenty-seven months. A UN peacekeeping force, the United Nations Verification Mission in Angola (UNAVEM), was set up to observe the phased withdrawal and monitor the cease-fire in Angola, parallelling UNTAG-Namibia, which would be doing the same as South Africa and SWAPO pulled their military forces out of Namibia.

The UN peacekeeping force was deployed and Resolution 435 was implemented as planned, including elections in Namibia in November 1989 and independence on March 21, 1990. Cuban withdrawal from Angola was completed in May 1991, five weeks ahead of the agreed schedule. By May 1991 Portugal, with creative help from the USSR and the United States, succeeded in brokering an agreement between the MPLA and UNITA on a cease-fire, elections, the end of outside military assistance, and so on. As in Namibia, there would be a central role for UN monitors and observers.

Analysis

As in the Congo situation, the United States was successful in its strategy and achieved most of its objectives in large part because of persistent, intelligent, informed diplomacy; the ability to understand and adjust to changes in the local, regional, and international political environments; and the sustained, top-level commitment of political will and material support. Linking Cuban withdrawal from Angola to South African withdrawal from Namibia and then engaging all parties actively in dialogue and negotiations was the specific key to success in this instance, since it gave each side something essential for its security and also something it could point to as a positive political benefit from withdrawal. However, the factors cited in the first sentence of this paragraph were essential in bringing about agreement, as was a close partnership with the UN. Officials were kept informed during the negotiations, and the parties counted on them to monitor and help enforce the agreements they reached. Equally important were the continuous consultations with regional African states and key Europeans, and eventually the bold decision by the Reagan administration to allow Cuba a place at the table. The United States was able to establish the essential modicum of trust with all parties, preserving it during periods of suspicion and gradually strengthening it as time went on. The United States demonstrated its top-level political commitment by its perseverance and the relentless intensity of its dialogue with all parties over a twelve-year period (plus two additional years until the 1991 MPLA-UNITA agreement was signed).

In the case of Angola/Namibia, as with the Congo, the general U.S.-USSR Cold War confrontation, the perceived threat of growing communist power and influence in many new African states, and the desire to roll back the communist threat gave the United States ample incentive for a sustained, highest level commitment to conflict resolution.

RECENT U.S. CONFLICT RESOLUTION ACTIVITY

Southern Africa

The serious U.S. interest and active involvement in southern Africa have been sustained up to the present in part through past momentum; in part because of a general Soviet eagerness in 1990–92 to cooperate with the United States in resolving regional conflicts (i.e., Nicaragua, Cambodia, and Iraq as well as Angola and Mozambique); and in part because of the importance of the region to the U.S. public and Congress, particularly in terms of resolving the black-white aspects of regional tension. A combination of the Black Caucus and more traditional liberal Democrats has continued to press the administration for action in Southern Africa.

The United States and the USSR supported Portuguese and UN efforts to broker a detailed political agreement between the MPLA and UNITA to stop the civil war, disarm militias, and hold elections. The 1991 agreement was endorsed by the Security Council and a peacekeeping force of 400 was approved to assist and monitor its implementation, including disarmament and a winner-take-all presidential election. The United States did not press for a more powerful UN role, nor did it take additional action to see that any agreement reached could or would be carried out successfully.

Militias were not disarmed before elections were held in 1992, and the elections were won by the MPLA but not accepted by UNITA. (Dos Santos appeared certain to be elected president, had a runoff election been held as required.) UNITA feared total exclusion from power and resumed heavy fighting to protect its interests. The lack of high-level understanding of the Angolan situation by the secretary-general and the Security Council, the failure to modify the agreement and the timetable to match the political-military realities on the ground, and the unwillingness of Security Council members (including the United States) to commit the much greater resources required for successful disarmament and elections contributed to the agreement's collapse and the return to civil war.

Subsequent efforts to restore the broken agreement have involved the United States, including an active congressional interest, but in a supporting or copartnership role with South Africa and the UN (and to a lesser degree Zaire), rather than the direct and active role played up until 1989. By working together to cut off outside support for UNITA and to reassure the MPLA, South Africa and the United States have made progress. Nelson Mandela hosted the Angolans in July 1994 and pressed successfully for new understanding. President Clinton has also been quietly involved, to the extent of exchanging letters with Angolan President dos Santos and appointing a special envoy (Paul Hare) who has worked actively with South Africa, the UN, and the Angolans. There are reasonable prospects that the new MPLA-UNITA agreement (the Lusaka Protocol of November 1994) will be implemented, even though it calls for UNITA to recognize previous elections and accept dos Santos's position as president until new elections are held at an undetermined future date.

For Mozambique, the negative lessons of Angola were learned and accepted by the UN secretary-general, the Security Council, and the United States. An agreement similar to that for Angola was negotiated in 1992 between the government in power and its chief opponent (RENAMO, which, like UNITA, had South African support). Sant'Egidio played the leading mediator role, together with the UN, supported by Italy, the United States, the USSR, and other interested governments. The Security Council endorsed the agreement, with provisions for disarming militias, elections, and so on and approved a peacekeeping force of 6,000 to 7,000. The United States fully supported this outcome, as well as later modifications, such as changing the timetable for elections to compensate for delays in disarming the militias and creating a new "retrained" national army. Refugees have returned in sizable numbers, many (but not all) militias have been disarmed and begun retraining for a return to civilian life, and elections were held successfully on October 27–28, 1994. The UN secretary-general, the Security Council, and the United States and other involved member states have shown a much deeper degree of political understanding in the case of

Mozambique than they did during the earlier Angolan situation. The United States has played an active and important role, although it is one of support rather than leadership.

The United States also took a keen interest in and provided low-key but active government and private assistance and encouragement to the eventual resolution of black-white conflict in South Africa. This manifested itself in myriad ways, involving NGOs, members of Congress, and other Americans. The Bush and Clinton administrations encouraged talks between the ANC and the government; facilitated meetings among President Clinton, Mandela, and de Klerk; gave advice and assistance on holding elections and drafting a new constitution; provided economic assistance; and encouraged U.S. private investment. While the United States was careful to avoid excessive interjection of outside advice and activity, there was no question that helping South Africa reach political agreement and make it work was a very high sustained priority for the U.S. administration and Congress, and it remains so today. This priority has powerful domestic popular and political support and has been portrayed as a successful policy achievement for the Clinton administration. Ironically, the emphasis on South Africa has come at some expense of attention and resources for other African problems.

Somalia

During 1991 and most of 1992, the United States resisted proposals that it become actively involved with the UN in Somalia, arguing that the UN was already overburdened. The United States led the effort in the Security Council in April 1992 to reduce the secretary-general's recommendations for 500 armed peacekeepers to assist humanitarian operations and monitor the cease-fire, instead approving only 50 unarmed monitors. The UN then authorized a 3,500-man force in August; only one battalion (Pakistani) went in (in late September), and it got pinned down or "stuck" at the airport. In August, President Bush took a much more active approach, catching up with the keen interest of the media (especially TV), a sizable group in Congress, and the NGO community. He authorized a large-scale airlift of food by the U.S. Air Force. This had little effect, and large-scale death from civil/clan war, famine, and disease continued, so the Bush administration decided to lead a multinational military operation and seek approval from the Security Council. In December 1992, twenty-three other countries and 10,000 forces joined the 27,000 U.S. forces in operation Restore Hope/United Task Force (UNITAF).

The Restore Hope/UNITAF phase of Somalia peacekeeping made tremendous strides in achieving its primary humanitarian mission, as death from malnutrition and disease virtually ceased. There was also an impressive beginning of political reconciliation, of bringing weapons and militias voluntarily under restraint in Mogadishu and other key locations, and of rebuilding local government structures and resuming agriculture and animal husbandry. It appeared that the United States and UNITAF had found a successful formula: overwhelming forces available for use at all times (with constant vigilance), used with maximum restraint and with every effort to limit the aftereffects; fulfilling the humanitarian mandate and showing the Somalis the advantages of peace; encouraging the Somalis to sort out their own problems and establish their own institutions, not taking sides or getting caught in the middle of their disputes and not imposing solutions on the factions; maintaining constant dialogue with all; and coordinating the implementation of humanitarian, political, and security/military activities to maximize and multiply their favorable impact. There was strong public and political backing for the operation in the United States and around the world. On the other hand, it was not widely recognized that the more traditional successor UN peacekeeping operation to UNITAF (UNOSOM II) would have a much more difficult time carrying out its broader, longer term mandate, which involved political reconciliation and disarming militias as primary missions, rather than protecting humanitarian operations.

In the spring of 1993, UNOSOM II, with strong U.S. political and military support, embarked on a more intrusive approach to political reconciliation and moved into first political and then military confrontation with the powerful Somali National Alliance (SNA) faction of General Aideed. Little effort was made to explain or develop popular and political support in the United States or other troop-contributing countries for this new mission. When inadequate understanding of Somalia's political dynamic and inadequate military resources for the new mission led to a war with the SNA (in which the latter killed some seventy peacekeepers and wounded three times as many, including ninety-six Americans killed and wounded on October 3–4), the backlash was sharp, swift, and inevitable.

In the United States it caused a confrontation between the administration and Congress, which resulted in a March 31, 1994, deadline to remove all U.S. military forces. A new policy emerged for the United States and the UN of accepting all Somali factions in the mediation process rather than rejecting one or another, putting the burden for agreement on the Somalis themselves and reducing the intrusive UN role. Going beyond Somalia, there was a pronounced turning away from positive administration attitudes and policies toward UN peacekeeping as the best means of dealing with "failed states" and the problems involving tens of millions of people caught up in humanitarian emergencies and civil strife. The administration and the U.S. military leadership also determined that U.S. military resources (personnel, equipment, and funds) would be used much more sparingly, reserved for more important U.S. interests, and that U.S. personnel would not be exposed to the risk of casualties unless truly vital interests were at stake. A similar, albeit less pronounced, cooling of enthusiasm for peacekeeping took place in a number of other countries, particularly in Europe.

Rwanda

When in late April 1994 the secretary-general called for a new UN peacekeeping force to try to stop Hutu-Tutsi genocide in Rwanda, the United States was initially opposed on grounds that what was proposed was poorly planned, uncertain of success, dangerous, and costly. Under pressure from the media and then from Congress, the United States accepted the idea but provided only minimal support. There was no prospect of an early or effective force, yet hundreds of thousands were being killed or fleeing the country. France could wait no longer and on May 23 undertook its own operation to set up a safe haven in southwest Rwanda. This action was endorsed by the Security Council just as the initial U.S.-led operation in Somalia had been, although only one other country (Senegal) joined France. Once U.S. television began to cover the hundreds of thousands of refugees pouring into Zaire, the administration decided on a major humanitarian response involving $300–400 million, 3,000 to 4,000 U.S. military personnel to reinforce hundreds of U.S. civilian (mostly NGO) relief workers, and a major airlift. This became part of an even larger international military and civilian humanitarian response. The new UN peacekeeping force was approved and began to deploy, although it was too small for its task, and a special representative for Rwanda was appointed for overall coordination.

For the 700,000 Rwandan refugees and the large relief operation in Zaire, international coordination is nominally the responsibility of the UNHCR. For humanitarian activities inside Rwanda, the responsibility is that of the UN Department of Humanitarian Affairs (DHA). For political and peacekeeping matters inside Rwanda, and nominally for overall coordination, the UN special representative is responsible. He is also trying to keep watch on Burundi, as well as the 20,000 to 30,000 armed Hutus from the former Rwandan regime who are living in Zaire. The difficulties and dangers of this situation and the uncoordinated international response are obvious.

Assistant Secretary of State George Moose has played an active role in consulting with all parties about the broader political aspects of the situation. However, there has been no high-level sustained U.S.-international leadership role on either political or humanitarian issues. The U.S. military was under strict orders not to become involved, even indirectly, in operations that could evolve into or be seen as peacekeeping or political, to limit its action to narrow technical humanitarian tasks, and to leave as soon as these tasks can be assumed by civilians. Rather than using the U.S. military presence to achieve broader secondary objectives, as part of an interlocking humanitarian-political-security strategy as was the case during Restore Hope in Somalia, the administration decided on maximum caution.

Other Countries

Donald Rothchild's excellent chapter (chapter 4) discusses several other situations in which the United States has been actively involved, at least at the State Department level, in seeking to assist conflict reduction; he also describes the different types of diplomacy used (direct, indirect, etc.). If one looks at Ethiopia, the Sudan, Nigeria, Zaire, Liberia, and Rwanda, it is evident that the United States has been limiting the degree of its involvement in African conflict resolution, other than that involving southern Africa. It is also evident that this limited involvement has been of some use. It often is a vital stimulus for the involvement of other governments and the UN, given the importance they attach to the United States as the only superpower.

Although it is very doubtful that the SPLA or the Bashir government will make any significant movement toward political agreement in the Sudan, President Clinton appointed a special envoy (Melissa Wells) to work with the east African leaders in IGADD to stimulate new negotiations and help them along. With the collapse of the latest IGADD talks, the next steps are uncertain. There is the potential for major civil strife in Nigeria over the 1993 elections, which the military regime refuses to accept, and the imprisonment of the unannounced winner, Chief Abiola. President Clinton sent Jesse Jackson as his special envoy (apparently on a one-time basis) in August 1994 to express concern over human rights, the restoration of democracy, and the possibility of major conflict. This visit produced no visible movement by the Abacha military regime, but neither has the feared explosion of political-ethnic violence taken place.

There is a great deal more that the United States could do for African conflict resolution, for example, more support for peacekeeping in Liberia and Rwanda. However, an increased U.S. role would require enough incentives for a more active administration role, which would also generate congressional support for increasing resources for Africa in the face of competing priorities, domestic and foreign. Without the Cold War and the special attention Congress attaches to southern Africa, this has not been the case thus far. In part because of the backlash by the public and Congress to Somalia—which has cooled administration ardor for rebuilding "failed states" and for "assertive multilateralism" as the means for so doing—and in part because of budgetary restrictions (including immense difficulties in obtaining a supplemental appropriation), the political will and financial support available for Black Africa has diminished sharply. Moreover, conflict resolution efforts other than those in southern Africa are competing for potential funds. The intra-African competition for resources comes from the increased number and magnitude of African humanitarian problems, often exacerbated, if not created, by civil strife. There is also stiff competition from Haiti (which tended to divert Black Caucus interest from Black African problems), Cuba, Bosnia, and other issues. Another obstacle to U.S. involvement in African peacekeeping is the severe strain on U.S. military budgets, which are already financing a number of unbudgeted activities such as care for Haitian and Cuban refugees and Rwanda relief.

Thus, the United States is providing no personnel and only limited material and financial support for the ongoing ECOMOG/UN operation in Liberia, although the operation is far from strong enough to resolve the conflict. The same is true of the Rwanda peacekeeping force, which is much too weak for its very difficult, dangerous undertaking. There has been no serious U.S. interest in a peacekeeping force for Burundi. The United States did, however, support the Angola peacekeeping force.

Final obstacles to greater U.S. involvement in African conflict resolution are the increased number of countries in which conflicts are taking place; the high incidence of civil or clan/tribe strife; the much larger numbers of people affected by this internal strife, which is often combined with and frequently causes or contributes to famine and disease; and the collapse or weakness of indigenous governments and administrative institutions. All this makes for more complex crises, with powerful interacting political, humanitarian, and security elements, crises whose resolution is much more difficult and dangerous. In Angola and Mozambique, there are governments and single, organized opposition groups with minimal capabilities and some discipline and cohesion while Liberia, Somalia, Rwanda, Burundi, and others that have broken into smaller pieces or where ethnic animosities are more extreme have proven even more difficult to resolve, and serious attempts to do so much more expensive.

CONCLUSION

The most obvious, simplistic conclusion is the urgent need for an organized, agreed-upon process of early warning and early response to African humanitarian crises as well as potential or actual civil strife. The United States and the key players in the international community, including concerned European and other governments and the UN network (secretary-general, Security Council, UNHCR, UNDHA, UNDP, UNICEF, World Food Program [WFP], etc.), must be part of this response system. The OAU and other regional African organizations, as well as key African governments for a particular crisis, should also be involved, as should the International Committee of the Red Cross (ICRC) and the worldwide NGO network. There is no question but that more large-scale humanitarian-political emergencies will occur in Africa in the years immediately ahead.

Given the frequency with which humanitarian crises in Africa are linked to civil strife and the causal relationships often found between the two, it is essential to bring the primarily humanitarian organizations into a much closer relationship with the primarily political organizations (including the UNHCR). There is also a vital need for contingency peacekeeping preparations, identifying and having available on short notice personnel, equipment, and transportation needed for most types of crises. Rapid action minimizes expense, peacekeeping casualties, and losses to the local civilian population. Equally urgent is the need for much greater and faster consultation and coordination in the decision-making and implementation phases by all the states and by the organizations mentioned in the previous paragraph. It is possible, under exceptional circumstances such as those that existed during the U.S.-led Restore Hope operation in Somalia, to bring about a reasonable degree of ad hoc coordination. However, this required an unusually assertive role by the United States and the cooperation of international organizations and NGOs on the ground, often without approval from their own headquarters and sometimes despite their reservations. This situation has not been replicated in the Rwanda crisis.

Another obvious conclusion is to improve the capacity of various organizations to respond effectively. The OAU has made only a minimal contribution to the crises in Rwanda, Burundi, Liberia, and Somalia, despite efforts by African governments, the United States, and others to get it to do so. The United States, other governments, and private organizations are working to build up the capability of the OAU, but it has a long way to go in acquiring the experienced personnel and financial resources needed for a systematic, reasonably effective conflict resolution program. There is also considerable reluctance among OAU member states to seeing the organization become overly active in what are perceived as primarily internal matters rather than as disputes between states. Even well-established organizations such as the UNHCR, UNDP, and the UN Secretariat have shown serious weaknesses in responding to the overwhelming problems coming out of Africa, where crises often develop rapidly and can involve very large numbers of people and a high degree of violence.

Together with and partly responsible for the limitations on the capability of international organizations to respond is the increasing reluctance by the United States and other major powers to take a leading role, much less a solo role. (France strictly limited the time and scope of its Operation Turquoise in Rwanda, much more than the United States did in Somalia. The United States has very strictly limited its Rwanda involvement.) Once a major humanitarian or political-humanitarian emergency has exploded, the prospects of high political as well as financial costs of involvement (especially where there appear to be no important national interests) are powerful deterrents to assertive action and material contributions from major powers.

Very early political and humanitarian action, preferably involving international organizations as well as key governments and NGOs inside and outside Africa, offers by far the best prospect of even limited success in dealing with potential or actual conflict situations. Skillful, rapid mediation and spelling out to the local leaders and people the prospect of rewards versus greater calamity can have a significant effect on the local political situation if the situation on the ground has not gotten beyond rational argument and where there is enough established authority with which to deal. This argues for identifying a "watch-list" of mediators from governments, international organizations, and NGOs with diplomatic skills and area experience, so that they can be called upon rapidly when a potential or budding crisis is identified. They will need to address the interlocking humanitarian-political-security elements of most African crises. The individuals selected should be supported or even taken on by international organizations such as the UN and the OAU, as well as by

African governments that have influence on the country or countries in crisis and command respect within the OAU (e.g., Ghana, Senegal, Zimbabwe, Ethiopia).

Similarly, peacekeeping units and qualified officers for command positions can be identified by key governments, the UN, and the OAU for potential crisis participation. Response time needs to be speeded up by advance planning for logistics, command and control, and so on, as well as readiness of troops and material for short-notice deployment. For the Congo and ONUC in 1960, the first UN forces arrived within forty-eight hours of the Security Council decision and the entire contingent of 10,000 was there within a week. For Restore Hope and Somalia in 1992, the first forces (United States, French, Belgian, Canadian) were there within two weeks of the U.S. decision and five days of the Security Council resolution, with over 15,000 on the ground within a month. So it has been and can still be done if there is sufficient political will to commit the resources. By better advance planning and pre-positioning, as well as better early warning and more rapid response, the size of the response force and the costs involved in deploying it can be very substantially reduced, as can the magnitude of the crisis for which it is being deployed.

Further, there is now a much greater need than there was during the Cold War period to generate public and political support for conflict resolution or conflict reduction in Africa, both before deciding to intervene and while the operation is under way. Without this support, either operations will not be politically feasible or they will risk being kept (or cut) very short, with inadequate resources. We have seen this with the United States and France in Rwanda, with the UN in Angola, and elsewhere. Combined efforts by the media, members of Congress (or parliament), the NGO community, and governments offer a reasonable prospect for generating and maintaining adequate support.

A final point is the need for active, visible, and consistent participation by the United States. Even when it is not advisable or there is not enough support at home for the United States to take the leading role, its active cooperation with others is extremely important. It often means the difference between whether they participate or not and also affects the position taken by the UN Security Council and other international and regional organizations. This does not mean, for example, that the United States must provide a large proportion of peacekeeping forces or most of the material support. It does mean that some U.S. forces should be part of a peacekeeping force (perhaps specialized units such as engineers, special forces, staff officers, or logistics), rather than the United States appearing to take a position that the mission is safe for others but too dangerous for us. We should be aware of the impact that the participation or nonparticipation of the world's only superpower has on others.

6

AFRICAN CAPABILITIES FOR MANAGING CONFLICT

The Role of the United States

Herman J. Cohen

"The United Nations must know when to say no." That statement to the UN General Assembly in September 1993 by President Bill Clinton was not an announcement of a new policy. It was the confirmation of a policy that had begun in early 1992 during the Bush administration. After the Cambodia peacekeeping operation was approved in 1991, and the price tag was announced as $2 billion, it was quite clear that a policy threshold had been reached. From that point, the United States and other large contributors were going to require the UN Security Council to be more selective in its approach to conflict, especially the internal variety that has been wreaking so much havoc in Africa.

Since then, the Security Council's slow and somewhat feeble initial approaches to the internal conflicts in Somalia, Burundi, and Rwanda have reflected the more cautious approach of the United States. The United States appeared to be willing to take an aggressive posture only in Angola, where it had a historical interest, allowing the Security Council to take a bold step in pledging as many as 7,000 UN peacekeepers to support a renewed peace agreement between the government and the UNITA movement, and in Somalia, where only a major U.S.-led military effort could stop the starvation in late 1992. The new atmosphere of selectivity and caution in the UN Security Council makes it imperative to look to regional solutions to regional conflicts.

WHERE IS AFRICA COMING FROM ON CONFLICT MANAGEMENT?

At the 28th Annual Summit of the OAU in Dakar in June 1992, African heads of state adopted, in principle, the establishment of a "mechanism for preventing, managing, and resolving conflicts in Africa," and asked the secretary-general to develop a plan for making such a mechanism operational. Following discussion and review at the Council of Ministers meeting in Addis Ababa in February 1993 and the Cairo Summit in the summer of 1993, the heads of state formally endorsed the mechanism at their Cairo meeting.[1]

The OAU's decision sent two important signals to the international community. First, the OAU was expressing the view that Africa must take primary responsibility for managing its own conflicts, thereby reflecting the reality of growing "conflict fatigue" outside of Africa. There was also an element of chagrin in this decision because it was becoming increasingly untenable for the Africans to observe the Americans, Italians, British, and other non-Africans taking the lead in addressing internal conflict in countries like Ethiopia, Angola, and Mozambique while African governments and NGOs did very little.[2] Second, the decision represented an important breakthrough in OAU doctrine, which had established the principle of noninterference in internal affairs as the most important element of regional cohesion. The 1993 decision to establish the conflict resolution mechanism reaffirmed the noninterference doctrine in very strong terms, but it was understood that all internal conflict in Africa would henceforth be fair game for OAU "interference" because African regional peace and security were clearly at risk.

In practical terms, the decision to establish a conflict resolution mechanism empowered the secretary-general to become an activist wherever and whenever he saw conflict emerging. He was no longer in a position of having to await orders from the OAU chairman or to be invited by an African head of state who felt in need of his services.[3]

A second significant effect of the decision was the collective pressure brought to bear on individual governments to accept OAU interference. Intervention is less of a diplomatic and juridical problem when the state and government either have disappeared or are in a state of near collapse as in Somalia and Liberia. However, whenever the OAU member government in a crisis country is still in place and is in control of at least the capital city, the OAU secretary-general still has to negotiate the organization into the picture. The fact that the conflict resolution mechanism was endorsed by consensus of the heads of state, however, makes it difficult for any government in trouble to refuse OAU inquiries and efforts to establish conflict management processes. The same holds true for insurgent groups and armed opposition, who find it difficult to refuse the OAU call to come to a meeting even when it is not in their tactical interest to do so.[4]

Finally, there has been an interesting change in the status of "legitimacy" of conflict protagonists in Africa since the OAU established the conflict management mechanism. Before that threshold decision, there was an implicit assumption in addressing all internal conflict that the government was the legitimate party and the insurgents, rebels, or armed opposition were the illegitimate party who nevertheless had to be dealt with through negotiations. This was perhaps to be expected because the OAU is, after all, an intergovernmental body. Two good examples of the illegitimacy of the armed opposition in African-led mediation were in Chad in 1977, where the northern rebels were considered surrogates of Libya in the context of an OAU peacemaking effort, and in Angola in 1989, where a negotiation chaired by Zaire began with the premise that the government would magnanimously make concessions to the UNITA rebels, who would dissolve their movement and merge into the preexisting one-party state. In Rwanda, on the other hand, the late Habyarimana regime failed completely to win acceptance of its argument that the RPF insurgency was essentially an act of aggression by neighboring Uganda. The OAU viewed the RPF rebels as the children of exiled refugees trying to come home.[5]

Two-and-a-half years after the U.S. intervention in Somalia (December 1992), the African landscape has evolved considerably with respect to conflict management. When mass starvation started in Somalia at the beginning of 1992, the Africans reacted by putting diplomatic pressure on the UN to take action. Now, Africans are in the forefront of negotiations and mediation in Somalia. Africans clearly have a collective will to take responsibility for conflict management on the African continent. However, Africa lacks the necessary resources, technology, and organizational capability. The international community, on the other hand, has seen its will to intervene in African crises erode considerably since Somalia (as much a result of increasing demands for costly intervention worldwide as the disappointments of Mogadishu). Nevertheless, the international community has the technology, resources, and training capability to help Africa take charge.

The question here is, what will it take to make an operational reality out of what appears to be a natural and mutually beneficial partnership?

THE AFRICAN EXPERIENCE IN CONFLICT MANAGEMENT: STRENGTHS AND WEAKNESSES

The few cases in which Africans have intervened without external assistance in an attempt to manage internal conflict have been analyzed quite extensively elsewhere by scholars such as William Zartman, Francis Deng, and Sam Amoo. So there is no need to repeat much of that analysis here. The same has been accomplished in analyzing the history of the OAU's generally unconsummated earlier efforts to establish functioning conflict management mechanisms (prior to the current effort, which began in 1992).[6] The story of the OAU's work on the Rwanda crisis of 1990 to 1994 has yet to be written, with much of the data confined to diplomatic channels. Nevertheless, I would like to review selected conflict management efforts for what they tell us about African institutional capabilities and weaknesses as opposed to why these efforts succeeded or failed.[7]

Chad

The OAU intervention in Chad ran from 1977 to 1982. It involved both mediation and the introduction of peacekeeping troops. The effort was not successful mainly because the original Chadian government led by Presidents Tombalbaye and Malloum saw the OAU as an ally in their fight against Libyan aggression rather than as a mediator with the internal opposition. When northern factions defeated the original southern-controlled government, the OAU was unable to mediate among them because they were determined to continue fighting until there was a victor and a loser. From the scholarly literature, it is clear that neither the OAU mediators nor the military peacekeepers had a clear mandate. They suffered from the pull of the government's legitimacy, and with respect to troop deployments from Nigeria and Zaire, this effort suffered from severe financial and logistical handicaps.

Liberia

The ECOWAS intervention in Liberia began in mid-1990 and continues to the present (June 1995). An ECOWAS Standing Mediation Committee effort began in April 1990 and almost reached common ground between President Samuel Doe and National Patriotic Front of Liberia (NPFL) rebel leader Charles Taylor. For a very short period, Doe agreed to abdicate the presidency if Taylor would agree not to capture Monrovia by force. After claiming that his only objective was to force Doe out, Taylor refused the ECOWAS deal, insisting that he must be allowed to take over the country and become interim president. In August 1990, twenty-five hundred troops from Nigeria, Ghana, Sierra Leone, Guinea, and Gambia entered Liberia in a task force called the ECOWAS Monitoring Group (ECOMOG). The immediate reason was the presence of thousands of non-Liberian West African nationals who were in danger of being taken hostage by Taylor's forces. The large number of Liberian refugees pouring into neighboring countries were also considered a threat to regional peace and security.[8]

ECOMOG's mission was both humanitarian and political: save lives, open up corridors for the distribution of food and medicine, and bring about a cease-fire leading to an interim government and a democratic transition. It can be argued that the operation was eminently successful in saving tens of thousands of people in the city of Monrovia from starvation. Large amounts of foodstuffs that were available nearby could not be distributed because of fighting in the city. ECOMOG lifted the siege just in time to avoid catastrophe. ECOMOG also pushed Taylor's forces far enough away from Monrovia to make it possible to install an interim government and begin serious negotiations. A number of observers, including journalists, have described the ECOMOG military intervention as a failure because the intervenors had to engage in combat to accomplish their mission. Those critics fail to discern the difference between peacekeeping and peace enforcement.[9] ECOMOG went into Liberia with the understanding that it might have to engage in combat to achieve its mission, and so it did when Taylor's forces resisted. That did not mean that ECOMOG was no longer a neutral party, even though Taylor tried to exploit the fighting to depict ECOMOG as partisan.

Serious negotiations did indeed begin under ECOMOG auspices and later under ECOWAS auspices, with UN assistance from a special representative of the secretary-general. These negotiations were long and arduous, but finally resulted in an agreement signed in Cotonou July 25, 1993, calling for a cease-fire, the installation of an all-party interim government, and elections in September 1994. While the agreement itself was reasonable, implementation has been very slow and troubled, with "warlordism" taking hold in a number of areas. The September 1994 election was not held, and prospects are poor for 1995 or 1996.

The ECOMOG operation in Liberia demonstrated that Africans have the will and the ability to organize relatively effective military interventions in both permissive and nonpermissive environments. ECOMOG in Liberia was a special case, however, because only oil-rich Nigeria had the resources to finance such a long military expedition with a minimum of outside assistance.[10] The fact that troops from five West African countries were able to operate in the same small area with minimal problems was also a positive element. Also, by using force, the ECOMOG units were able to demonstrate their ability to take measured actions with limited objectives. There is irony in the fact that the ECOMOG operation appeared to deteriorate in effectiveness after the Cotonou agreements, which transformed ECOMOG from a peace-enforcement operation to a peacekeeping one. Reports of corruption and partisanship among ECOMOG troops since Cotonou are apparently reliable.[11]

The ECOWAS contribution to a search for a Liberian solution was also noteworthy beyond the military aspects. In effect, the ECOWAS mediation committee demonstrated a persistence and mediating skill that led to the Cotonou agreements after a long and frustrating period of negotiations.

The Rwanda Crisis: The OAU's Faltering Efforts to Take Charge

When the Rwanda crisis erupted in October 1990 with the arrival of RPF forces from Uganda, the first international reaction was from France, which dispatched troops to Kigali to prevent the RPF from achieving a quick victory. Subsequently, most of the work leading to a cease-fire and the Arusha accords of August 1993 was organized by the OAU, with leadership provided by President Mwinyi of Tanzania. The OAU also provided fifty cease-fire monitors who were actually deployed with the help of external financing. The process broke down completely in April 1994 when extremists in the Habyarimana government embarked on an anti-Tutsi campaign of genocide that devastated Rwanda and unleashed destructive forces that were not controlled until early 1995. When it came to monitoring the Arusha accords, however, the OAU lacked the resources and capability, which made it necessary for the UN Security Council to deploy twenty-five hundred UN blue helmets.

The Rwanda experience has demonstrated some interesting aspects of the OAU in relation to conflict management. First, in deploying monitors for cease-fires or similar situations, the OAU can call on a considerable reservoir of military officers and units that have had extensive experience in UN operations, both in Africa and in other regions. The African countries that have done the most in this area are Nigeria, Senegal, Kenya, Botswana, Ghana, and Zimbabwe. Second, it is clear that even for small operations like the deployment of fifty monitors, the OAU does not have the financial resources to go it alone. Third, when it comes to larger operations, such as the UN deployment in Rwanda, the OAU can work only with the UN as the senior partner. Finally, the OAU's modus operandi in conducting political negotiations is to appoint a neighboring chief of state, such as Tanzania's Mwinyi in the Rwanda crisis, to conduct a mediation effort. Again, this method demonstrates the OAU's lack of resources, since the lucky regional neighbor has to take on the expensive burden of hosting the talks, which usually drag on. Thus, while the negotiations are African led, the OAU sponsorship is usually forgotten by both Africa and the international community.

In some cases, subregional organizations are given the OAU assignment to conduct negotiations. The Sudan negotiations are currently being conducted under the auspices of IGADD, which consists of the nations of the Horn of Africa. As mentioned earlier, ECOWAS was in charge of the Liberia talks. During a breakdown of governance in Lesotho in January 1994, it was the members of the Southern African Development Community (SADC), including the new South Africa, that took the lead in restoring order and stability to that country. These examples make it clear that when the international community is developing a conflict management partnership with Africa, the subregional organizations must be taken into account along with the OAU.

The Lone Ranger Approach: Intervention by a Head of State or Eminent Person

Occasionally, an individual head of state or eminent person seeks to intervene in a conflict situation without reference to the OAU. For example, before his fall from grace in September 1991, President Mobutu of Zaire had the stature to conduct Angola negotiations in 1988 and 1989. He was unsuccessful. In the Congo, by contrast, President Omar Bongo of Gabon was very effective during 1993 and 1994 in defusing internal political tensions and stopping the nightly combat in Brazzaville between various armed militias belonging to different political parties.

These examples illustrate the significance in Africa of the respected individual who is always senior in both age and longevity as a political leader. Those leaders with financial or military clout in addition to seniority, such as Bongo of Gabon, Moi of Kenya, or Mandela of South Africa, carry added weight into such negotiations. This is the reason these personalities tend to become involved in conflict situations more than the others.

This influence of these leaders should be considered in any potential African conflict management program. Among eminent African persons who are not in government but have attempted to do third-party mediation are Archbishop Desmond Tutu of South Africa and General Obasanjo, former head of state of Nigeria.

In Summation: The African Institutional Record

African efforts in conflict management to date have shown strengths in negotiation, mediation, and traditional peacekeeping in permissive situations, particularly those military establishments that have extensive experience in UN operations. There have been very few African experiences with military operations in nonpermissive situations. In Liberia ECOWAS managed military units from five West African nations under Nigerian leadership and did a competent job. But this experience is not likely to be repeated because of the high cost. Any further operations will have to be under UN auspices. Nevertheless, Liberia showed that it was possible for Africans to handle nonpermissive situations in Africa without non-African leadership.

The OAU's conflict management mechanism is a long way from being operational. Problems with organization and personnel are so severe that the OAU has not been able to fully utilize funds made available by donors in 1992, 1993, and 1994. Until the mechanism becomes fully operational, the OAU will have to delegate negotiations to regional leaders of stature and delegate military operations to the UN. Nevertheless, with the breakthrough in OAU doctrine concerning noninterference in internal affairs, the OAU has a mandate to become involved with internal conflict. Carrying out this mandate will require sufficient resources, organizational capacity, and qualified people.

The options of calling on regional African leaders to lead negotiations and calling in the UN to conduct peacekeeping operations will always be available and will undoubtedly always be used. It will be especially important to keep the regional leaders engaged in the process. A fully operational conflict management mechanism, however, will be able to give full support to mediators in the form of trained experts as well as logistics and administration, which are now absent. A fully functioning mechanism will also allow the OAU to stay with a conflict situation much longer than at present, possibly making calls to the UN less frequent.

For the longer term, Africa's internal conflict will not be resolved by the short-term political-military measures envisaged for the conflict management mechanism. The threat of violent internal conflict can be diminished in African societies only when political culture in Africa can develop nonviolent means of settling differences of opinion created by conflicting political and economic interests. Only when all ethnic and regional groups feel they are not threatened by the political power structure will the threat of conflict fade. That is why political liberalization and good governance must go hand in hand with conflict management.

THE INTERNATIONAL COMMUNITY: CAPABILITIES, ASPIRATIONS, AND HANG-UPS

The American Dimension: Multilateralism versus Neo-Isolationism

In his annual speech to the UN General Assembly in September 1992, President Bush discussed the "new international order." His speech was made in the context of the end of the Cold War, Operation Desert Storm in Iraq, twelve ongoing UN peacekeeping operations around the world, and the daily reports of starvation coming out of Somalia. He spoke of a world in which conflict would be managed through multilateral mechanisms, with unilateral interventions such as the U.S. invasion of Panama no longer acceptable. He also revealed that he had issued a directive to the Department of Defense ordering the revision of training manuals to include substantial training time for conducting peacekeeping operations. He ordered that the service schools include this subject in their curricula and that multilateral peacekeeping become a career specialization in the military.[12]

President Bush's statement was consistent with his policy in the Iraq-Kuwait crisis, when he insisted on a UN Security Council resolution under chapter VII of the UN charter authorizing a U.S.-led military operation against Iraq. When he decided to intervene in Somalia in December 1992, the same procedure was followed. The United States asked for and was granted a UN authorization to undertake an operation in Somalia.[13]

President Clinton came into office in January 1993 with enthusiasm for multilateralism as the vehicle for conflict management. He expressed strong support for Bush's intervention in Somalia. After the tragedy of October 3, 1993, when sixteen U.S. soldiers were killed in Somalia, the U.S. political mood changed, and the Clinton administration had to assume a more cautious approach toward both multilateral intervention in conflict and U.S. participation in conflict management. In a policy directive identified as PDD 25, President Clinton said that the United States would selectively engage its forces and resources in overseas conflict situations linked to U.S. vital interests. In addition, the United States would use its considerable influence in the UN to prevent the Security Council from being profligate and imprudent in its interventions. It is not surprising therefore that the United States imposed considerable restraint on the UN Security Council when it initially considered intervening in crises in Burundi in 1993 and Rwanda in 1994.[14]

Despite the caution and selectivity in the Clinton administration's approach to conflict management abroad, the medium-term trend toward multilateralism and restructuring of the military for peacekeeping operations continues to deepen in U.S. policy. Military services are increasing their doctrinal orientation and training to make conflict management a major element in their missions. At the same time, the administration is calling for multilateral peacekeeping funding to be divided between the State and Defense Departments to provide for more realistic budgets and greater flexibility. The administration appears to be ready to support a partnership between Africa and the international community if the result might be a diminished demand for U.S. forces and a more equitable level of burden-sharing.

Non-American Industrialized Country Training Activities

The Canadians, the Nordics, the Dutch, the Irish, the French, and the British all have a lot more experience in using military forces in conflict management than the United States. This is especially true in training for peacekeeping operations, which require far different skills from combat training. According to a recent study commissioned by the Henry L. Stimson Center, a number of industrialized countries have established in-depth peacekeeping training programs. The Joint Nordic Committee for United Nations Military Matters (NORDSAMFN) appears to have the most sophisticated and extensive training capability. Other countries undertaking similar programs include Ireland, Luxembourg, Germany, the Netherlands, Spain, and Switzerland. Of special significance has been the formation within NATO of the Ad Hoc Group on Cooperation in Peacekeeping, whose mission is to promote common understandings of the political aspects of peacekeeping and to develop common practical approaches. Canada has already established the Canadian International Peacekeeping Training Center.[15]

The policies of most of the non-American industrialized countries are essentially favorable to multilateralism and generally in favor of UN leadership in conflict management. The training capabilities they have established, or are in the process of establishing, indicate a potential area for north-south cooperation with Africa.

WHAT DO THE AFRICANS WANT, AND WHAT DO THEY NEED?

The beginning of wisdom among African leaders is the knowledge that in matters of conflict management, Africa cannot go it alone. In their decision to establish a "mechanism for conflict prevention, management, and resolution," the African heads of state in 1993 decided that the OAU would concentrate on early warning, conflict prevention through rapid diplomatic intervention, peacemaking, and peace building. Major operations such as postconflict peacekeeping and peace enforcement (e.g., Somalia) would have to be the responsibility of the UN, with strong African participation.[16]

Two years later, the OAU mechanism exists and has demonstrated energy in becoming involved in internal conflict. The OAU has worked in South Africa in monitoring and mediating political conflict, has sponsored President Bongo's mediation in the Congo, and has sent monitors to both Rwanda and Burundi. On the basis of its work to date, the OAU has established the important precedent that internal conflict is the concern of all of Africa. Staff work for the conflict management mechanism is being provided by the OAU's political department until a full-time staff can be recruited to work exclusively on conflict. Leadership direction is provided by Secretary-General Salim Salim himself. For the moment, the ability to plan, network, and organize operations is essentially minimal. On the basis of statements made by Dr. Salim Salim and some of his colleagues, a fully functioning mechanism would have the following characteristics:

- A separate department of the OAU secretariat, with a director reporting to the secretary-general.
- Three sections: preventive, planning, and military operations.
- Earmarked contingents in African national armies, trained in peace observation and peacekeeping.[17]

Because its work is so unique, it would probably be important to establish the mechanism as a separate department of the OAU, staffed by proven African experts in the field of conflict management, including military operations. The need for the mechanism to be operational twenty-four hours a day and to react rapidly would argue for the importance of a separate department under the leadership of an assistant secretary-general.

If the OAU members can find the financial resources to pay recurring costs such as salaries and allowances, it should be possible to find dynamic Africans with experience and knowledge of conflict situations to staff the new department. Seed money for organizational requirements, including training, the provision of technical assistance, and equipment such as communications gear, is already available, and more should be forthcoming from donor countries. The United States, for example, has already made $9.5 million available (FY 1992 to FY 1995), and legislation enacted at the end of 1994 authorizes funding for a variety of conflict management activities in Africa. For FY 1996, the administration requested $29.61 million for conflict resolution, peacekeeping, and military training in Africa, including $5 million to assist the conflict resolution activities of the OAU.[18]

Probably the most important short-term need will be for technical assistance in operational planning, military planning, and administration of external assistance. For the medium term, assistance will be needed to train Salim Salim's "earmarked contingents in African national armies." According to the Stimson Center study cited above, Africa joins the Middle East in having the least training of both military and civilians for conflict management.[19]

It is significant that the OAU is not thinking solely in terms of mediation and intervention in conflict situations. At the annual African heads of state summit in Tunis in June 1994, there was extensive discussion of the issue of general security of nations, with particular emphasis on governance, liberalization of politics, participation in decision making by all ethnic groups and regions, and decentralization.[20]

OUTLINE OF A PARTNERSHIP FOR CONFLICT MANAGEMENT IN AFRICA

If the Africans are serious about wanting to assume responsibility for their own conflict management, and if the international community is serious about wanting to support Africa in reaching this goal, then the outlines of a partnership arrangement are discernible. Let us look at such an arrangement as a set of mutually reinforcing commitments from both Africa and the international community.

African Commitments

1. Build and maintain an early warning and prevention network covering every country in Africa.[21] The early warning system would maintain current information on confrontational situations that appear to be moving

toward an impasse and possible violence and where internal mediating mechanisms appear to be failing. The prevention system would maintain a network of volunteer mediators and intervenors who would be willing to provide good offices in an effort to reduce tensions and unblock confrontational political situations. The network could be coordinated within the OAU conflict management mechanism or independently through an NGO network or a new organization created expressly for this purpose, working in connection with the OAU and subregional organizations.

2. Agree that all internal conflict in Africa would automatically be the subject of external interest, concern, and possible diplomatic intervention. Doors would always be open to OAU conflict management inquiries.

3. Expand or reconfigure the OAU secretariat to provide for adequate staffing of the conflict management mechanism headed by an appropriately experienced director, or even a newly created assistant secretary-general, reporting directly to the secretary-general.

4. Agree to work toward a threshold date when all African conflicts would automatically be addressed initially by African institutions only, with other players coming in only when called on by Africans.

5. Agree on the designation of five African combat battalions that would be dedicated to conflict management operations and would be kept in readiness for such operations at all times. These battalions could be called on either by the OAU or by the UN to be used in conflict management operations of various kinds.

6. Set up a core group of ten African heads of state who would serve as an emergency steering committee that could respond to urgent requirements on short notice. The ten heads of state should be connected by special hot-line telephone or telex satellite links.

7. Make a collective determination to eliminate the basic causes of tension through political liberalization, improved governance, and greater citizen participation in decision making. Such a determination would serve as continuing peer pressure on regimes that fail to move in the right direction and therefore become vulnerable to tensions and conflict.

8. Accept an "African" rate of support payments to African troop units for peacekeeping operations in Africa. The standard UN rate of approximately $900 per month per soldier is far too expensive for African operations. As its contribution to a partnership, Africa should accept a lower rate for operations in Africa by African military units.

International Commitments

1. Provide assistance to the OAU conflict management mechanism in the form of technical assistance (to be furnished mainly by African experts) and appropriate equipment pursuant to plans formulated by the OAU itself.

2. Include African military units in peacekeeping training offered by donor countries and the UN.

3. Give military assistance to Africa. Used during the Cold War to support "friends of the West" regardless of their human rights record, military assistance to Africa is now on the wane because there is no longer a geopolitical purpose. Military organizations, however, are a major element of internal conflict. They need to be transformed into leaner establishments whose main mission is to support democracy. Military assistance is probably more important now than it was during the Cold War.

4. Undertake to support the training and equipping of the five African battalions dedicated to conflict management operations in Africa.

5. Undertake to support an African conflict prevention network to be organized by African NGOs in cooperation with the OAU and African governments. Provide short-term training to develop capacity in mediation and other conflict management skills.

6. Consider making Africa the pilot region for the implementation of the UN Agenda for Peace proposed by Secretary-General Boutros Boutros-Ghali in July 1992.[22]

RECOMMENDATIONS FOR U.S. POLICY

The partnership proposal described above should appeal to U.S. policymakers for two reasons. First, U.S. peacekeeping troops can be deployed abroad only where America's vital interests are in jeopardy. This is unlikely to be the case anywhere in Africa. On the other hand, U.S. humanitarian assistance is always available to Africa in ever-increasing amounts, even though such assistance invariably turns out to be more expensive than early preventive intervention. Second, budgetary constraints prevent the U.S. government from acquiescing in every proposal for UN peacekeeping.[23] The only solution is to establish a system within which the Africans will form the front line of defense against conflict within Africa itself. If properly organized and financed, this front line should be able to dispose of most conflicts by catching them early. Only the most difficult and intractable situations would be subjects of international action by the UN or other systems. If this concept can be made operational and if the Africans themselves move courageously down the road to democratization, then the overall costs to the international community and to the United States should diminish over time. The initial U.S. investment in helping the OAU conflict management mechanism and related conflict prevention networks would appear to be worthwhile, especially in comparison with the vastly higher costs of addressing humanitarian crises when they are at an advanced stage (e.g., Somalia, Rwanda).

The U.S. Track Record

As far as Africa is concerned, the United States has displayed a keen interest in helping the Africans develop their own institutional capacity for conflict management. The U.S. government has probably done more than any other in this area.

The United States has judiciously made both the OAU and ECOWAS eligible for nonlethal military assistance through presidential determinations. United States aid to ECOWAS and to Senegal for the Liberian conflict was substantial, although it was far less than the actual cost to Nigeria, the prime troop supplier. U.S. assistance to the OAU conflict mechanism amounted to $4.5 million for FY 1992 to 1994. In October 1994, Congress enacted legislation that authorizes a variety of assistance to Africa for peacekeeping and conflict prevention. Beyond assistance to the OAU conflict management mechanism, the United States is also a leader in the broader area of assistance to democratization and governance in Africa through the auspices of the U.S. Agency for International Development (USAID) and the U.S. Information Agency (USIA).

One place where U.S. policy can be questioned for its lack of foresight and wisdom is at the United Nations since early 1992. American reluctance, based as much on budgetary reasons as any other, to support early and vigorous UN action in Somalia (1992), Burundi (1993), and Rwanda (1994) probably condemned both the United States and the entire international community to larger than necessary humanitarian relief and military operational outlays. The mistake that the U.S. government appears to be making at the UN is to equate multilateral action to manage conflict with U.S. bilateral action. The United States appears to be subjecting both the bilateral and the multilateral options to the same criteria. Needless to say, this line of reasoning will make it harder than in the past to use the United Nations even when it is appropriate.

Suggestions for U.S. Policy

Make the OAU operational: The United States should continue its good work in supporting OAU efforts to operationalize its conflict management mechanism. Funds have been made available. An activist, dynamic ambassador who knows the issues and who is strong on administration and budget is in place in Addis Ababa. An additional defense attaché has been assigned to Addis to spend most of his time on OAU liaison. The ball is in the OAU's court to take advantage of available assistance and expertise in order to come up with workable plans and proposals.

Bring back military assistance: This is difficult considering budgetary problems and the negative attitudes in the 1990s. Nevertheless, there is an important potential role for military assistance in the prevention and management of conflict. Armies must be downsized and retrained to support democracy rather than repression. They need training for international peacekeeping duties. The U.S. military knows Africa well after three decades of active involvement in military-to-military cooperation. Its involvement in changing Africa's military would be most welcome and useful against a backdrop of conflict avoidance and management. Such assistance could be carried out without an iota of lethal equipment being transferred. What is needed is training, organization, and nonlethal equipment.

Give coherence to UN policy: The United States appears to be of two minds when it comes to multilateral activities in the area of conflict. It wants the UN to undertake tasks that the United States itself is reluctant to do. But America is reluctant to see the UN act independently of U.S. policy. The United States criticizes the UN bureaucracy for inefficiency but provides little leadership to straighten it out. The U.S. tendency to apply the same criteria to UN involvement in conflict as it does to its own involvement is a formula for gridlock. Recommendations for U.S. policy with respect to the UN are as follows:

- Exert leadership in the Security Council to enhance UN conflict management capabilities.
- Support the designation of Africa as the pilot continent to implement the Agenda for Peace.
- Resolve Africa's arrears problem in the peacekeeping account.
- Strengthen the UN's role as a coordinator of international peacekeeping training.
- Formulate a policy for UN intervention separate from the one governing U.S. intervention.

- Support the reform of bureaucratic procedures in the UN to permit rapid responses to crises.
- Support the creation and proper staffing of a UN coordination center for conflict management.
- Encourage African subregional organizations to become active in conflict prevention and management in their own regions (i.e., SADC, ECOWAS, IGADD).
- Give "civil security" the highest priority in all U.S. bilateral relations with Africa.[24]

Adopt a continent: Within NATO, three militarily powerful members know the African military scene well as a result of decades of military cooperation—the United States, France, and Great Britain. NATO needs to find creative new roles as it downsizes and reorients itself. The U.S. European Command, whose commanding general is also the supreme commander of NATO forces, has always had African military cooperation as one of its major responsibilities. The French take their military cooperation with Africa so seriously that responsibility lies in the Ministry of Development Cooperation rather than the Ministry of Defense. The British also have significant ties with Africa through training and assistance to African Commonwealth countries.

Between September 1994 and March 1995, the British and French governments were in contact with the OAU on the subject of training and equipment for an African stand-by military contingent. The OAU has responded positively to these overtures. The British and French are emphasizing African cooperation with the Western European Union, which would have the virtue of including Germany, Belgium, and Portugal, all of which have military assistance programs in Africa. It would have the disadvantage of excluding the United States, however. Both France and the United Kingdom have kept the United States informed of their initiative, and have indicated an interest in coordinating their activities. With military assistance funds in short supply in all donor countries, all donor contributions are welcome. Placing a coordinating office in NATO would serve the same purpose, and would have the advantage of including the United States.

Continue to support political liberalization and good governance: The United States is a leader in supporting democratization and improved governance in Africa. Such programs should be continued and reinforced within USAID. In addition, the budgetary process should recognize that

USIA has a major role to play in promoting democracy in Africa. This agency has the proven capability and the appropriate techniques, and it should also get a significant share of the money. Only when substantial improvements in governance lead to greater popular participation in daily decision making and to greater fairness and justice for all regions and ethnic groups will conflict be settled through nonviolent means in Africa.[25]

7

GUIDELINES FOR PRESERVING PEACE IN AFRICA

I. William Zartman

Conflict management cannot be forced on conflicting regions, nor are African conflicts the responsibility of outside powers. Yet, left to their own devices, Third World regional conflicts force their way onto global agendas, at times and in terms not in our interest or to our liking. The most striking, obvious, incontrovertible lesson of recent conflicts and peacemaking efforts, from Africa or elsewhere, is that left untended, conflicts grow worse, requiring efforts vastly more costly and wasting incredible numbers of lives. Inaction is bad policy both for the people engulfed in the conflict and for the leadership position of the primary superpower.

Leadership, as any CEO knows, is not a matter of direct intervention and micromanagement, but of guidance, coordination, and inspiration. Thus, an American policy of cooperative security and preventive diplomacy does not mean acting as the world's gendarme (in the familiar, denigrating phrase) but rather enabling, supporting, galvanizing, and backing collective activities. Some actions should fall directly on the United States; others are best performed by others; all should be coordinated. To give a specific example, it was a wise decision for the United States not to be the intervenor in Liberia. Africa needs experience in handling its own conflicts, even at the cost of making mistakes in the process. The correct American role was to help fund the ECOMOG operation, enabling the Senegalese and later the Ugandans and Tanzanians to join, and to join in providing UN backing for the regional states' response.

Yet an additional and legitimate concern must be addressed: While the catastrophes of current history could all have been avoided or attenuated by early action (and early warning was clearly available in all cases), many similar cases did not become catastrophes. Catastrophes demand early intervention (in the broadest sense), but not all early warnings indicate catastrophes. How can early warnings that will turn into catastrophes be distinguished from those that will not? While that question cannot be answered usefully in a single rule, it will be important to keep it in mind through the following discussion. The notion of early warning has been much overused and confused in its two senses. There is plenty of advance intelligence on upcoming crises and simmering conflicts, and there is as yet no sense of scientific models and indicators (as in meteorology) on which to rely. The real problem is when and how to react.

Taken together, these considerations mean that American peacemaking policy in Africa should above all focus on mobilizing and supporting the collective responsibilities of the African states themselves, operating through the OAU and the subregional organizations (SROs) such as ECOWAS and the West African Economic Community (CEAO) for francophone states, SADC, and IGADD, among others. The possibility of providing "layered responses," where one agency can pick up the problem when another becomes bogged down, is an advantage to be used in the contemporary world. It is not necessary or desirable for the United States to intervene directly in all African preconflict and conflict situations, although in some situations its presence may be required. Policymaking therefore necessitates separating situations of direct involvement from those in which the United States serves a number of indirect roles, from animator to funder to mediator or intervenor of last resort. Policymaking also necessitates close, active, ongoing coordination with European states with special interests in Africa. Most measures cannot be taken by the United States alone and certainly not by the United States in opposition to French or British policy.

Since space is not available here to present an analytical history of recent African conflicts, we will go directly to conclusions that can serve as a basis for discussion. Looking back, each crisis indicates some early action following an early warning that could have changed history. An effort by

African neighbors within IGADD, with outside powers' backing, to hold a conference of local forces in Somalia in early 1991 would have gone far to save hundreds of thousands of lives and billions of dollars. External and African support for Mobutu's retirement when his term ran out in 1993 would have saved the fragile Zairean democratic movement from grinding destruction and the state from impending collapse. Coordinated African pressure, backed by the UN, on Rwanda and Burundi to accept monitors to help implement and observe their reconciliation and democratization measures would have gone far to save hundreds of thousands of lives. Effective disarmament, a substantial international peacekeeping force, and a power-sharing outcome would have attenuated the Angolan conflict. U.S. refusal to endorse the fraudulent 1985 elections in Liberia, coupled with support for the opposition and for a smooth transition to the real winner, could have obviated the Liberian civil war.

Many other examples can be proposed and debated, but it is more constructive to consider specific measures the United States can take to help in conflict prevention and reduction.

STANDARDS FOR DEALING WITH CONFLICT

Africa needs its own principles to uphold. The most important and most delicate effort needed is sustained pressure on the OAU secretariat and member states to establish some norms and standards for dealing with the causes and manifestations of conflict. The OAU has been extraordinarily effective in inhibiting irredentism by its doctrine of *uti possidetis;* it needs to turn the same norm-building efforts to democratization (respect for election results, tolerance of opposition, independence of the judiciary) and sovereignty (responsibility for one's own minorities).

Happily, an African proposal addressing these specific issues and others is already on the table in the form of the Kampala Document for the CSSDCA, sponsored by General Olusegun Obasanjo. The OAU adopted conflict prevention, management, and resolution mechanisms from the document in 1993 and 1994 but has not adopted the principles and standards that should guide these mechanisms. Such guidelines are needed; they are obviously beyond the direct reach of U.S. policy, but western support for the Kampala Document and pressure for its adoption would be useful. The congressional Commission on Security and Cooperation in Europe would be a useful player.

AFRICAN CAPACITY-BUILDING

Capacity-building for Africa in peacemaking and peacekeeping is the most economical and appropriate path to effective conflict reduction. American efforts and funding can most fruitfully be devoted to this area, rather than waiting for the mad excitement of crises. Capacity-building takes two forms—support for long-term institutionalization and support for immediate actions.

Institutionalization needs are dual and complementary. The OAU and subregional organizations need a supportive intelligence capability (something many African states' foreign offices do not have). The function would be not so much a 24-hour operations center as an information and documentation center with a small, alert staff to supply background memory, preventive diplomacy doctrine, and current intelligence to a troubleshooting team. The organizations also need senior diplomats available to intervene on an informed basis to cool mounting tensions; yet such people are likely to be chosen for their knowledge of the situation and peacemaking practices and are unlikely to rely much on an information center. An ongoing partnership between the two, built on successive experiences, is important; institutionalized support is useless without a skilled diplomat. Mohammed Sahnoun's mission to the Congo in 1993 is a good example of an effective intervention.

The U.S. contribution is already in place in the unusually farsighted efforts of the House Foreign Affairs African Subcommittee in providing support to the OAU for its conflict prevention, management, and resolution division in 1994 and 1995, with provision for support to SROs as well. It is too early to draw lessons or judge effectiveness. Support to cover the expenses of diplomatic missions would certainly be welcome, given the state of the OAU and SRO budgets, particularly in the subregional cases, where all such efforts are ad hoc.

Immediate needs are more visible. The most important is to build an African capability for peacekeeping operations that would give useless armies a purpose and provide a common, continental experience in upholding agreed-upon norms. A side benefit is that African troops, not U.S. or French troops, would be handling African conflicts. The most immediate need is for logistic support. It is truly incredible that, as of May 10, 1994, the OAU secretary-general had obtained troop contribution commitments for Rwanda from eleven African states, but four months later none of them had arrived for lack of transport, whereas in 1978 the United States was able to arrange transport for French troops to Shaba within forty-eight hours. It is far better to ferry African troops early than to send in U.S. troops several hundreds of thousands of deaths later.

There will be a lot of on-the-job learning in such operations, but all in all the conduct of African troops in the multinational operations in Shaba in 1977–78, Chad in 1981, and Liberia in 1991–94 was not bad. It would not be inappropriate to use military training assistance to establish common training programs for members of the same SRO to prepare for such operations and to minimize military adventures at the same time.

DISARMAMENT AND DEMOBILIZATION

Arms and armies are the means of conflict; disarmament and demobilization are the ways to remove those means. It is clear from Angola and Somalia, and it is now being relearned in Rwanda, that other measures of humanitarian and peacemaking policy are built on sand if the conflicting armies are allowed to sit by and watch, weapons in hand. It is also clear that disarmament is lengthy and costly, and that it is likely to be imperfect and incomplete, but these should not be excuses for not doing it at all. The UN disarmament and demobilization policy in Mozambique is exemplary, even if it has holes. This is not the place to go into the details of disarmament and demobilization, which are well known. The point to be emphasized here is the prior element: A commitment to the process and to bearing the costs of removing arms and disbanding armies is necessary.

REBUILDING STRUCTURES

Handling conflict is not simply a matter of restoring order through peace-keeping forces; it means rebuilding state structures once peace is restored. The Somali experience, with potential calls from Angola, Mozambique, Liberia, Rwanda, and Zaire, show that African states in the process of collapse often need emergency assistance in reestablishing their civil structures after the peacekeeping force has finished its work. Military forces are needed to restore security so that government and society can function again, but often the mechanisms of civil society and administration are destroyed in the ravages of conflict. Standby measures are needed to provide for ready assistance, yet they pose the same problems that plague military intervention.

One solution would be the formation of reserve units of "blue hats," who would train as "weekend administrators" and be ready to serve when the UN Security Council issues the call. These reserve administrators would operate in much the same way as military reserve units (including military government units) that are available for call-up when U.S. forces are required for military operations or, in some other countries, when assignments for UN blue helmets are issued. Blue hats' functions could include police, health and hospital, post and telecommunications, local government, education, and other types of administration. They could be organized as part of the military reserves or national guard under the Department of Defense or as a new venture under the State Department. The Inspectors Corps of the United Nations is currently working on a similar proposal.

COALITION-BUILDING

Building new coalitions is an important part of conflict management and state reconstruction. Experience has bounced from one clear "lesson" to another, but coalition-building is not an easy task. Initially, it was thought that an early return to the people through elections should produce a clear winner with a popular mandate, as shown in the Zimbabwean experience, among others. The Namibian experience showed the value of mixed results and cooperation among competing parties; the Angolan experience then showed that a winner-take-all outcome was a formula for rejection, which led to the understanding that elections should establish only the proportion of participation in a power-sharing arrangement, an outcome that the South African experience seemed to support.

While this is an appropriate conclusion, it does not answer the initial fears in Angola of a power-sharing government paralyzed by participants with knives in their pockets. Power-sharing alone is not the full answer, and there is no magic formula for making it work. The biethnic nature of the RPF in Rwanda and the multiethnic nature of the council in Somaliland were promising conditions, but they do not tell how to overcome the problems of long hostility among the parties in Somalia, Angola, or Mozambique. Without the willingness to reconcile and cooperate, the only measure to make power-sharing work would seem to be an international representative—optimally a UN secretary-general—backed by a monitoring force to make the process as transparent as possible and to keep conflict management on track until it can run on its own. The actions of the

UN representative in Nicaragua and the monitoring process in El Salvador are relevant here.

DEALING WITH ROGUE FACTIONS

Rogues and warlords are a part of the problem that need not be part of the solution. Somalia, Rwanda, Liberia, and even Angola pose the vexing problem, for which clear solutions are hard to find, of appropriate measures to take toward international "outlaws" who directly challenge the international community's peacemaking and peacekeeping efforts. The matter raises some very serious problems that are not easily answered. There is no single guideline, but a few rules may make the problem more manageable.

On the one hand, on a strategic level, the name of the peacemaking operation is reconciliation, the establishment of a set of fair rules of operation and institutionalization under which the new system can run. Containing rogue forces within such a set of rules is more important than punishment and more likely to create a new system rather than perpetuate cycles of revenge. International efforts should avoid conducting a war against one side or another and instead should seek to draw all sides into a cooperative arrangement. To leave the Habr Gidir or the Hutus or the Krahn or the Ovimbundu out of a new political system in their countries is a formula for failure.

On the other hand, on a tactical level, when a specific incident involves a military attack on international forces, it should be responded to in equal measure, not by a ranging foxhunt for the political leader but by a carefully planned and targeted strike against a specific unit of his forces. Its planning, execution, and backup are military questions of importance.

Whether war crimes trials, such as those recently launched in Rwanda and Ethiopia, are warranted in these cases is a difficult question. Such measures make peacemaking negotiations more difficult, but they may remove the need for revenge or blood payments and therefore actually facilitate reconciliation. Where the threshold lies to activate the trial process and who should be indicted are questions with no easy answers. If such trials do occur, they should be held under the auspices of an international organization in the country, not by the new government. It may be that a public information process, as carried out in El Salvador, is better and sufficient. Whatever the form, such measures should be undertaken in conjunction with the establishment of continentwide norms. Including Africa in the international concern on these matters will reinforce Africa's efforts to establish legitimate structures of authority.

DEMOCRATIZATION

Democracy is a process, not a state of perfection, and its meaning is philosophical as well as operational. African societies are caught up in the wave of democratization, and incumbent rulers do their best to retain control in the storm. Democracy is not measured merely by free and fair elections, or even by fairly contested elections, any more than it depends on alternance—bringing in the opposition or throwing out the incumbents. Democracy is government carried out by democrats, by politicians committed to society's right freely to choose and freely to repent its previous choice, without punishment. Democratization is a learning process, a process of improvement over past practices, not simply a matter of being democratic or not.

The United States needs to be clearer in its statements and explanations about democracy and democratization, providing both inspirational and operational guidance for African states seeking to consummate their struggle for national self-determination. In Algeria, the United States has deplored the cancellation of elections about to be won by a party that promised it would hold no more democratic elections. In Zaire, it has sought compromise with a dictator who has consistently repudiated his own agreements with a struggling democratic movement. In Angola, an election that produced a winner also produced a loser capable of overthrowing the electoral process. Explaining the subtleties of democracy and the gradual process of democratization is no easy task, and African opinion, ever suspicious and too prone to conspiracy explanations, is quick to see in democratization the political equivalent of structural adjustment, an imposition from outside. Democracy needs to be related to Africans' concerns and practices, and championed more comprehensively in America's official statements.

ESTABLISHING BOUNDARIES

Boundaries are a major cause of African conflicts. While African boundaries are frequently held to be artificial, they are no more so than any other boundaries. Drawing lines through any human community is artificial, and no boundaries anywhere coincide neatly with ethnic, geographic, social, and economic divisions. Africa's problem is that its boundaries are recent and therefore need to be "Africanized"—made part of the life and history of the individual African states and societies. If this is not done by the time-honored ways of war, it must be done by equally established means of diplomacy. One major technical weakness of African boundaries with a comparatively easy solution is the fact that though most are delimited (defined on a map), many are not demarcated (marked on the ground).

Some African states have made it a point of their foreign policy to demarcate their boundaries with their neighbors. In the process of demarcation, neighbors can often discover and resolve anomalies and ambiguities that, if left unattended, could be the cause or excuse for conflict in times of worsened relations. Outside powers, no matter how well intentioned, cannot push African states to demarcate their borders. But they can provide technical assistance and training in demarcation to enable African states to pursue the Africanization of their boundaries. An American program for this activity would be a specific contribution to the prevention of conflict.

SUPPORT FOR CONFLICT MANAGEMENT

Very few Africans study, analyze, teach, or write on the various aspects of conflict management, reduction, resolution, and prevention. There is no ready context for thinking about ways of reducing conflicts among African states and no ready community of support for policies of handling conflict across borders. African diplomats have been creative and active, but without any organized backup for their work. More broadly, African societies almost universally lack a public forum for the discussion of foreign issues. Such conditions are signs of a developed society, but they can also be part of the development process and need not await a higher stage of development to be instituted. Both types of institutions can be fostered by the United States, possibly with the help of other interested countries.

It would be useful to promote the formation of a group of African experts, from inside and outside government service, to meet regularly with American and other specialists in conflict management and to develop a common language and sense of community in support of such practices throughout the continent. The goal would be to set up an experience somewhat similar to the Dartmouth Conferences of the Kettering Foundation, but devoted to African conflict management, not to U.S.-African relations. The Brookings Institution's African Studies Program, in conjunction with the Johns Hopkins University's School of Advanced International Studies and other similar programs, has considered such an activity, but it needs support and organization. The Global Coalition for Africa has also made efforts in this direction.

Similarly, the development of public forums for discussion of foreign and especially inter-African relations among civic leaders in and out of government is a basic requirement for an informed democracy, not a luxury of development or an elite club. Tunisia has an Association for International Studies but the rest of the continent has very little activity of this kind. African countries need their own councils on foreign relations to raise awareness, promote free discussion, and help build bridges between the African intellectual community and African policymakers. The Council on Foreign Relations based in New York could be instrumental in helping African countries create their own bodies, if given appropriate support.

CONCLUSION

The causes of conflict in Africa remain, and its incidence can be expected to rise. The most important lesson from the spotty American experience is that it needs to show decisiveness and leadership in helping Africa handle its conflicts; expanding and supporting Africa's efforts is more important than intervening directly. The continent needs to improve its mechanisms for dealing with rising conflict, lest the impending changes in norms on boundaries, noninterference, state integrity, and governance, added to continuing structural rivalries, tear the continent apart. A frank look at the OAU and its proposed parallel structure, CSSDCA, plus increased attention to regional and subregional mechanisms for conflict management, is needed. The front line of conflict management, however, is conflict prevention through defended norms, demarcated boundaries, democratic practices, and active diplomacy.

8

INSTITUTIONAL CAPACITY-BUILDING FOR AFRICAN CONFLICT MANAGEMENT

Summary of the Discussion

Timothy D. Sisk

O bservers of conflict in Africa rightly focus on the large-scale humanitarian tragedies resulting from the civil war and internal violence that have befallen, and continue to befall, some African states. Anarchy in the streets, untold battlefield deaths, hunger, and massive civilian refugee flows and displaced persons attract and deserve a response from the international community, either to prevent further escalation of strife or to meet the humanitarian needs of the victims of war. Yet virtually all analysts of the African scene recognize that the longer term answer to managing conflicts is to improve the capacity of African institutions at regional, subregional, national, and local levels to manage tensions and mediate disputes without recourse to violence and armed insurrection.

A new, post–Cold War theme of "layered responses" to African conflicts is emerging in which local and national organizations respond first, with subregional and regional organizations—and eventually the broader international community—following as needed to prevent a conflict's escalation.

Local actors such as states, NGOs, or regional or subregional organizations may be able to deal with small-scale crises through mediation, conciliation, and negotiation assistance, particularly with diplomatic and material support from the international community. Only when a crisis has gone beyond the capacity of African institutions to respond should the international community consider a more intrusive role. Above all, close coordination among myriad actors at all stages of a conflict is required for successful peacemaking, peacekeeping, or peace-building.

As African states undergo profound social transformation and political transitions in the post–Cold War era—which some have called a "second independence"—new opportunities for institution-building have arisen that give practical meaning to the notion of layered response. Many proposals have been put forward for creating new institutions or enhancing the capability of existing institutions, and some have begun to be implemented. Some options are grandiose and ambitious, such as the creation of a powerful African security council. Others involve less significant, but nonetheless important, structural changes, such as introducing conflict resolution curricula and degree programs in African universities.

Increasingly, U.S. policymakers are searching for ways to improve the indigenous capacity of Africans to resolve conflicts. As Ambassador Melissa Wells, former U.S. special envoy to Sudan, argues: "Our aim should be to strengthen Africans to take primary responsibility, then build the secondary rung in terms of the international community."[1] Many elements contribute to the theme of institutional capacity-building to promote conflict management: policy initiatives to bolster the OAU's peacemaking ability and to improve its linkages with the United Nations and other international organizations; support for peacemaking or peacekeeping by regional organizations; helping to undergird negotiation processes to end civil wars; emphasizing democratization—especially forms of postelection power sharing—and sustainable development; and nurturing civil society in African states. These initiatives should be supported by diplomatic efforts, aid flows, and occasionally, in the most serious and tragic crises, military intervention.

Based on the discussion at the symposium, this chapter reviews a number of options for institutional enhancement in Africa and surveys some of the advantages and disadvantages of these options. The chapter concludes with a review of the U.S. role in enhancing the opportunities for institutional capacity-building to promote the routinized management of conflict in Africa through legitimate and effective institutions.

REGIONAL INSTITUTIONS: THE ORGANIZATION OF AFRICAN UNITY

The Organization of African Unity, established in May 1963, was not considered an effective instrument of conflict resolution during the Cold War despite some occasional successes in mediating conflicts related to border disputes. African conflicts were entangled with superpower rivalry. With the end of the Cold War, however, African states and the international community alike seek to devolve peacemaking responsibilities to regional organizations, and regional organizations seek to enhance their role in their own affairs in coordination with the peacemaking and peacekeeping activities of the United Nations. Indeed, the OAU has become increasingly involved in peacemaking efforts in internal conflicts, including Liberia, Burundi, the Congo, South Africa, Mozambique, and Angola.

In that spirit, the OAU created in 1993 a Mechanism for the Prevention, Management, and Resolution of Conflicts. In the short time since the establishment of the mechanism, the OAU has deployed preventive diplomacy missions under its rubric. An observer mission has been sent to Burundi, for example, to prevent the spillover of the Rwandan conflict. Calls abound for fully operationalizing and enhancing the capacity of the mechanism to anticipate and resolve conflicts in Africa, and for the creation of new regional institutions. Some of the options being considered at the regional level include the following.

Improving the Mechanism: Early Warning and Preventive Diplomacy

The most immediate emphasis on institutionalizing conflict management in Africa is bolstering the mechanism's role in collating information that can provide early warning of impending violent conflict and suggesting potential preventive intervention strategies that can forestall its outbreak. The current vision is that the mechanism would provide intelligence for the OAU secretariat, which would act on the information. Many analysts recognize that the central problem in Africa, and globally, is translating credible early warnings into effective diplomatic action.[2] Olara Otunnu, president of the International Peace Academy, argues that "the problem on the whole is not the gathering of information and in many cases . . . the conveying of information, but how you translate information which is available into concrete initiatives."

In terms of capacity-building, however, operationalizing the mechanism's intelligence function is a prerequisite to a regular and reliable flow of information that could lead to preventive diplomacy. But the OAU has concerns that may inhibit the mechanism from becoming fully operational and effective. One is the fear that the international community, particularly the UN, would become too assertive and seek to control the functioning of the mechanism, meaning that African states would lose their collective sovereignty. A second is that the mechanism may overshadow other OAU institutions, such as the central organ, which according to the OAU charter have primary responsibility for promoting peace and security. The ultimate concern about the mechanism, however, is that it may become—for some member states—too effective, undermining the sovereignty of regimes or the perceived prerogatives of parties to a conflict.

An African Security Council

Because of concern about the mechanism's potential, some have called for the creation of an African security council, along the lines of the one proposed by Mazrui in chapter 2. Specifics vary, but the basic idea is the same: the creation of a standing group of ten to fifteen relatively influential African states that could meet quickly and act decisively to intervene in a crisis—a true collective security system. Proponents of the notion suggest that African crises are so severe and the current response mechanism so inadequate that new institutions are required. Although the mechanism provides for regular meetings in Addis Ababa of a core group of fifteen African ambassadors (backed by the foreign ministers), which could function as a type of security council, proponents of a new institution suggest that it would be a quantum step toward a more powerful regional organization capable of dealing with the continent's crises. Mazrui's proposal differs from others in that the four permanent members—Ethiopia, Nigeria, Kenya, and South Africa—would have powers in some ways analogous to those of the five permanent members of the UN Security Council.

Detractors suggest that the OAU is already hostage to the interests of powerful states—such as Libya, Sudan, Zaire, and Nigeria—that are themselves embroiled in conflict. An OAU security council, much like the existing OAU institutions, would be ineffective precisely because it would be reduced to the lowest common denominator of a single powerful state. Edmond Keller of the University of California, Los Angeles, suggests that such a council would have an especially difficult time dealing with "regional hegemons" with ambitions and actions inimical to the interests of their neighbors. For that reason the creation of such a security council is seen by some as distracting from the principal task of implementing the mechanism.

Some express an even more ominous concern about the proposed security council. By enhancing the collective power of already powerful African states, the door is left open for inter-African colonization or annexation. For this reason, many smaller or less powerful African states would feel threatened by such a new institution, and thus its creation does not appear imminent. What is most needed, critics such as Keller argue, is a fundamental rethinking of the bounds of state sovereignty and the conditions for intervention, an issue that must be clarified before new institutions like the mechanism can be truly effective.

An African Senate or Council of Elders

Another proposal, also posited by Mazrui, is the creation of a pan-African senate or council of elders. Mazrui prefers the notion of a senate, because it can give former heads of state, for example, life after the statehouse. These eminent persons, with their experience and knowledge, would be available to work with parties to prevent or resolve disputes. Others, such as Zartman, prefer the notion of a council of elders because it may be a more feasible goal. Indeed, the Nigeria-based African Leadership Forum has proposed the creation of CSSDCA, which would include the establishment of a pool of statesmen-mediators. Creating the CSSDCA is an attractive option to many analysts because it can also serve to establish a set of consensus values, or yardsticks, by which to measure the performance of member states.[3]

Detractors of the senate or council idea question whether many African former heads of state, some of whom were not fairly elected or did not govern responsibly, should be rewarded with a position of high influence and status. Moreover, they would not have the moral authority required of a group of eminent persons whose task is to mediate among warring factions. Another concern is that an eminent person or persons could in fact undermine the mediation efforts of states, subregional, or regional organizations by being too conciliatory with aggressors or providing some form of legitimacy that other mediators have withheld. With that concern in mind, Herschelle Challenor of Clark Atlanta University has suggested that Africans should consider the creation of an elected parliamentary entity within the OAU—similar to the European parliament—that would serve a similar peacemaking function and would also counteract the "executive preeminence" that she believes characterizes the politics of the OAU.

An OAU Peacekeeping Force

Despite disagreement on institutional changes for the OAU, there is considerable consensus that the OAU is presently ill equipped, or ill prepared, to launch regional peacekeeping missions on its own. This realization was reinforced by the tardy response of the international community to the tragedy in Rwanda. Although African states provided the lion's share of the UN peacekeeping force—United Nations Assistance in Rwanda (UNAMIR)—that was deployed after unilateral French intervention, the OAU was unable to take overall responsibility for the operation. African states such as Nigeria, Ghana, Tanzania, Botswana, and Senegal do have significant experience in UN peacekeeping missions, and some larger states—Egypt, Nigeria, and South Africa, for example—have considerable military capabilities with regard to logistics, communications, manpower, and equipment. One proposal is to put the experience and capability of these states at the hands of the UN in a more structured fashion when peacekeeping is needed, for example, to implement a settlement in Angola or Liberia. Although not an official OAU function, an informal group of states on call would significantly improve the ability of Africans to participate in peacekeeping missions on the continent.

Next to peacekeeping, a perhaps more immediately realizable goal that has been suggested for Africa is the creation of an "African Peace Corps" or "blue-hat" force that—with the participation of other members of the international community—could be engaged in peacemaking, peace-building, and development work in Africa. Such a corps could augment, or have an adjunctive relationship with, the civilian administrative assistance that Zartman describes in chapter 7. This group would be especially useful in instances in which national governments have collapsed and a long-term period of rebuilding is required, such as in Somalia, Rwanda, and Liberia.

The list of possibilities to promote conflict resolution in Africa is not limited to the above. Some have called for an African high commissioner for refugees and an African court of human rights or African court of justice, for example. The debate about the efficacy of these options mirrors closely the consideration of the new institutions described above, namely whether new institutions should be created or whether the existing institutions should be infused with new energy and resources.

SUBREGIONAL ORGANIZATIONS: PEACEKEEPING AND PEACEMAKING

African subregional organizations, once considered somewhat irrelevant to peacemaking, have of late come into the spotlight in terms of their role in conflict management. Beginning with the intervention by ECOWAS in the Liberian conflict in August 1990, subregional organizations have assumed tasks not envisioned in their founding charters. The ECOWAS intervention in Liberia was initially seen as a potential model for the new role of these institutions in subregional conflict management. In the early months of the Liberian intervention, the fighting ebbed and a promising negotiating process began. External powers, including the United States, supported the ECOWAS initiative with financial and military assistance and diplomatic initiatives to achieve a sustainable cease-fire, as described by Cohen in chapter 6 and referred to by Rothchild in chapter 4.

Since the initial period of success, ECOMOG (the ECOWAS peace-keeping force) has experienced myriad obstacles to achieving its mandate, including internal dissension among contributing states and military setbacks on the ground. Peacemaking efforts were also stalled throughout 1992 and 1993—despite a more formal mediatory role by the OAU beginning in mid-1992—and the civil war remained stalemated throughout much of 1994. Richard Joseph, of the Carter Center, notes that "ECOMOG forces had to pull back that year from what used to be called greater Liberia. . . . So after everything that has been done, obviously we have to consider that exercise a less-than-successful one." This point is reinforced by other analysts. Robert Mortimer suggests that "although ECOMOG may yet emerge as a forerunner of future ventures in African regional conflict management, its own mixed results illustrate once again that intervention in civil war is a perilous undertaking and peace an elusive goal."[4] Another cease-fire of uncertain stability was reached just before Christmas 1994, and the ECOMOG experience will continue to be an important example of both the possibilities and problems of regional initiatives supported by the international community.

A second example of subregional institutional involvement is the new-found role of the East African regional organization IGADD in mediating the conflict in Sudan. Institutionally, IGADD has been ill-suited to serve as a mediator, but considerable attention and effort have been paid to bolstering the organization's capability.[5] It is much too early to judge IGADD's adventure into regional peacemaking, given the military stalemate on the ground and the apparent unwillingness of the parties to negotiate in good faith. IGADD is presently seen as the best vehicle to break the Sudanese impasse because the mediating parties—neighboring states, led by Kenya—have a direct interest in regional stability.

The strong interest of neighborly mediators in achieving stability was also behind the third recent example of peacemaking by subregional organizations, when members of SADC launched an effort to reverse the decision by Lesotho's monarch and military to oust the recently elected parliament.

South African president Nelson Mandela and Zimbabwean leader Robert Mugabe led efforts to calm the situation in Lesotho and to keep a nascent democratization process there on track. Similarly, southern African regional leaders were extensively involved in the UN/OAU-mediated talks in Lusaka, Zambia, to broker a new peace in Angola. These talks also were successful, producing a detailed settlement in late 1994 along with a commitment by regional actors—especially South Africa—to participate in a newly invigorated, two-year UN peacekeeping operation in Angola.

The southern African experience in regional peacemaking—as well as the experiences of ECOMOG and IGADD—may portend a general conclusion about the promise of subregional organizations as peacemakers, despite their principal role of fostering economic integration and development. Because of an overriding interest in their neighborhood's stability and their actual or potential leverage with disputants, subregional organizations may be uniquely qualified to launch preventive diplomacy efforts, to effect a change in attitudes that leads to viable and sustainable negotiated settlements in cases of civil war, and to help ensure complete implementation of agreements.

STATE INSTITUTIONS AND CONFLICT MANAGEMENT

Noting that most conflicts in Africa are internal civil wars or insurrections, many based on the grievances of ethnic minorities or majorities, attention has rightly been placed on the role of the African state in mediating ethnic conflicts. Virtually all African states are multiethnic states, a legacy of colonial arbitrariness in the demarcation of boundaries. Those states that are considered relatively homogeneous—such as Somalia—are beset by sub-ethnic cleavages that may produce equally dangerous violence. The extent to which a state unfairly distributes resources among groups, therefore, is a critical indicator of actual or potential conflict. Many analysts suggest that the most important task for conflict resolution in Africa is to create viable, legitimate, democratic states that distribute resources fairly and thereby mediate intergroup tensions. This is especially important as many African states have experienced profound transitions toward multiparty democracy in recent years.[6]

The most popular policy prescription by external parties seeking to promote intergroup accommodation in democratization processes—including U.S. and UN policies—is power sharing, in which all significant groups in society are represented proportionally in a postelection coalition government.

Power-sharing agreements are encouraged to flow from negotiated settlements in the course of democratization, through pacts in which the prospects of a winner-take-all election are mitigated by assurances that all parties will have positions in the coalition government commensurate with their vote share in an election. The democratization pact reflected in South Africa's November 1993 constitution, as well as the negotiation process that produced it, is often cited as an example for other African states to emulate.[7]

Power-sharing pacts should not be seen as a panacea, however. Some, such as Gerald Bender of the University of Southern California, suggest that external pressures to form national unity governments after an election can portend second-class democracy in that there is little opportunity for opposition and therefore a lack of accountability. Rather than encouraging a grand coalition at the top, Bender suggests, the United States and other external parties can encourage constitutional arrangements that allow for a proliferation of power. For example, an opposition party can gain power at the regional level through either elections or negotiated settlements, even though it may have lost a national election. Advocates of power-sharing acknowledge the concerns about a "grand coalition" government but nevertheless see it as a transitional or "democratizing" device. Zartman suggests, for example, that "it is inappropriate to expect that rules for a [democratic] process that has been operating for a very long time should apply to a process that's being set up for the first time. . . . The power-sharing notion is important . . . in building up the kind of consensus that is necessary for democracy to prosper over a longer period of time." Despite its potential problems—lack of accountability, the difficulty of "cohabitation" with erstwhile enemies, and the continued unwillingness of parties to accept losing an election—power-sharing is still attractive in transitional settings.

Symposium participants emphasized not only the process of democratization, but the institutionalization of democracy in terms of constitutionalism—the creation of legitimate, widely accepted rules of the game. As Pauline Baker of Georgetown University suggests, "Power-sharing agreements are agreements that are short-term. . . . Constitutionalism really represents a bringing together of the parties to define the functions, structures, and processes of the state and its citizenship in the long term." She adds, "Coalition governments in and of themselves don't work in Africa. And why? Because they don't go the next step and talk about the constitution and what happens after the first election."

Transitions to multiparty democracy are one potential source of conflict amelioration, but some analysts consider the failed-state syndrome to be an even more important issue. It is necessary to differentiate between these situations because the policy prescriptions may be quite different. Rwanda, Somalia, and Liberia are the best examples of failed states, but the waning capacity of other African states such as Zaire or Algeria to control territory is seen as an important and even greater challenge than transitional situations. Crawford Young of the University of Wisconsin views the distinction as critical, for while African institutions may be capable of shepherding transition processes, the failed-state syndrome is far beyond their capacities and may well require a collective response by the international community—including, possibly, military intervention. In large states such as Zaire or Nigeria, Young suggests, the required response will be "way beyond the OAU's capacity to respond . . . [because] the possibilities of mayhem are much greater in scale."

BETWEEN THE INDIVIDUAL AND THE STATE: CIVIL SOCIETY AND NGOS

Perhaps the area on which agreement among analysts is broadest is the appropriateness of a role for civil society in the management of conflict in Africa. Civil society organizations can and will continue to play a critically important role in two respects: intervention by NGOs at a "track two"—or unofficial—level to promote conflict management, and analysis and understanding of conflict and its potential amelioration.

Increasingly, NGOs are becoming involved in early warning mechanisms and in launching preventive action, as well as in integrating principles of conflict resolution into development and humanitarian relief programs and other peace-building chores such as military integration and demobilization.[8] With the massive humanitarian relief efforts in Africa in recent years, beginning with the 1984 Ethiopian famine relief initiative, action-oriented NGOs have become increasingly significant players on the African scene. Many of these organizations are international but hire significant numbers of local staff, who tend to be on the front line in hot conflict situations. Although most NGOs enter a conflict situation with a relief or development mandate, they quickly become involved in conflict mitigation, in part because a relative degree of security is a prerequisite for their tasks. Indeed, the lines between humanitarian relief and conflict intervention have become blurred over time, and some combatants and analysts alike suggest that emergency relief can sometimes exacerbate conflict and actually fuel fighting.

NGOs tend to be internationally organized and led, or nationally organized, but there are few truly regional NGOs in Africa, with the notable exception of the All-Africa Conference of Churches, which has mediated a number of disputes. For this reason, Herschelle Challenor encourages the development of an indigenous relief organization capacity in Africa, specifically a pan-African relief organization. Training and initial support for Africans could be forthcoming from the many international relief organizations that have participated in the massive operations mounted in Africa in recent years. Proponents of this idea, such as former Ambassador Melissa Wells of the State Department, suggest that it may also have a side benefit: encouragement of a grassroots spirit of pan-Africanism.

NGOs with a specific conflict resolution mandate have emerged in several African states in recent years. For example, a number of organizations providing conflict mediation services became very important during South Africa's transition from apartheid to democracy.[9] The purpose of these NGOs is to provide conflict resolution skills training as well as to intervene in disputes to promote intergroup reconciliation. Some, such as those in South Africa, have experienced clear success. Local NGOs in Africa may bring a particular advantage to peacemaking efforts: They are knowledgeable about the complexity of local conflicts, and they enjoy the confidence of local community and church leaders, so they may be able to effect change such as social rehabilitation and reconciliation that national, subregional, or regional organizations cannot.

According to some analysts, however, dependence on civil society institutions as potential conflict resolvers can go too far. Herschelle Challenor argues that "universities, labor unions, and private sector NGOs . . . should [not] be given a greater role in mediation because they are accountable to no one. I think you need people involved in mediation who have to be accountable to a broader public." An additional concern about African NGOs is their questionable "nongovernmental" character. Because many receive funding from the state, their independence can be called into question. One suggestion for bolstering the independence of both operational and analytic NGOs is to remove their dependence from state revenue by at least one step, perhaps by affiliating NGOs with universities, where they may still receive some governmental support but with fewer strings attached.

Civil society institutions are also critically important for generating knowledge about conflicts and their resolution. A number of institutions within Africa—including those in Nigeria, South Africa, and Kenya—seek to provide the "intellectual rudder" for international conflict management that some analysts contend is absent. Bethuel Kiplagat, for example, is concerned about the "divorce in Africa . . . between the government and the civil society, such as universities, in terms of exchange of ideas." But these institutions have limited impact because, as Guy Martin of Clark Atlanta University suggests, "there must be a linkage or bridge between the political establishment and the academic community which does not exist at the moment." Michael Chege of Harvard University, who strongly supports creating a greater capacity for policy analysis in Africa, is also concerned that the problem does not lie on the supply side of the equation, but rather on the demand side. "The most difficult problem," he suggests, "is that you might supply research findings to a policymaker, but you can't make him think. . . . Until our leaders understand the analytical outputs of research institutions, we're in big trouble . . . [this is] a question of leadership."

Some suggest that one way to bridge the gap is the proposal, put forward by Zartman in chapter 7, to create something akin to an African council on foreign relations. Detractors doubt that such a group can actually influence policy, suggesting that African leaders are by and large immune to input from nongovernment interests because of the extent of power consolidated in centralized, essentially patrimonial states. They suggest that until the accountability of political leaders is improved, no amount of collegial interaction will positively affect policymaking.

Cultivating leaders receptive to analytical inputs from civil society is a long-term challenge, yet analysts are virtually unanimous that African universities—from whence new leadership would emerge—are in a state of serious decline as a result of mismanagement, a lack of resources, and neglect by political leaders. Some allege, too, that the policies of international development institutions tend to favor basic or secondary over tertiary education, thus compounding the problem. In addition to improving the basic infrastructure and quality of African higher education, some suggest that a long-term strategy for enhancing the capacity of Africans to manage conflict is to introduce conflict resolution curricula and degree programs—teaching skills of negotiation, problem solving, mediation, and conflict analysis—in African universities. In the long run, too, strengthening NGOs in civil society can help build popular support and create constituencies that put pressure on governments to adopt accommodative policies that minimize the outbreak of violent ethnic conflict.

CONCLUSIONS FOR U.S. POLICY: POSSIBILITIES AND CONSTRAINTS

The challenge for the United States in exerting a leadership role in helping Africans develop the institutional capacity to manage conflict, according to analysts of U.S. policy toward Africa, is to recognize, as Chester Crocker put it, that the premise of "pay now or pay later" underlies the policy framework. If the United States and the international community neglect emerging conflicts in Africa and fail to engage in early efforts at conflict management, disputes may well escalate into the types of humanitarian tragedies that have been witnessed in Somalia and Rwanda, which go far beyond the current capacity of Africans to handle. Once that occurs, and knowledge of the human suffering that is a consequence of these conflicts becomes popularized through intensive media coverage, public opinion produces a desire to respond, usually at a much higher level of engagement—including military intervention—with its commensurate high costs. How can U.S. policy get away from being "CNN-driven" toward a more coherent and concentrated effort to help Africans build the institutional capacity to manage their own conflicts?

There is a strong consensus among analysts that the United States must work at all levels *simultaneously* to help create a viable institutionalized mechanism for response to conflict in Africa. Although the United States will continue to engage the OAU directly, U.S. policy should be designed to support the other layers of institutions—subregional, national, and NGOs in civil society—to help Africans create a viable conflict management system based on the layered response concept.

The layered response concept, as debated by symposium participants, is further elaborated by two principles: the division of labor (or comparative advantage) principle and the coordination principle. The division of labor principle suggests that different types of intervention by suitable actors at different stages of a conflict's escalation are most cost-effective and successful. All layers of the response mechanism must be capable of intervening when their involvement best bears fruit. The coordination principle involves ensuring that each layer in the response mechanism is working cooperatively and in concert with other layers. For example, a U.S., UN, or OAU preventive diplomacy mission should not undercut the locally sensitive work of an NGO, and vice versa.

Consistent, coherent, and sustained U.S. leadership at all these levels will be required if the United States is to contribute to the institutionalization of conflict management in Africa, according to Chester Crocker. He notes: "Leadership is more than direct action, certainly more than direct combat action. It is more than being out in front of everybody else. It means aggressive, behind-the-scenes coordination with key partners in Europe, in the Middle East, in Africa to use whatever leverage we can get to create a broader burden-sharing basis so that African governments, African regional organizations, the OAU, and NGOs can come to play their proper leadership roles. Let's engage and let's recognize how essential it is that we do so in our own interests."

James Woods, a former Department of Defense official, agrees: "We are going to have to be sophisticated enough, or open-minded enough, to see all of these things working together and cutting across one another and hopefully reinforcing occasionally, rather than colliding with one another." As other chapters in this volume point out, the place to begin is with the day-to-day work of U.S. diplomatic missions in the field in support of African peacemaking initiatives. Andrea Young, a congressional staff member, suggests that "the real advantage of . . . focusing on the behind-the-scenes support role of the United States is you have an opportunity to achieve a little more consistency and avoid some of the whipsawing that we get when issues only come to the attention and only come to a decision when they're . . . on CNN, when emotion is driving the policy."

However, the question of how—precisely—to implement the coordination principle is the matter foremost in the minds of policymakers. As Ambassador David Shinn, director of the Office of East African Affairs at the State Department, has asked: "How do you engage these groups more effectively? How do you get more of them involved on the ground? Do you work through the OAU directly, and do they in turn work with these groups? Do you create more of these groups, funding them directly? What is the way to bring the local groups more effectively into the policy process?" Answering these questions suggests that much still needs to be done to clarify the notion of layered response. These answers also suggest what the United States can do to promote a functioning response mechanism.

There are clear possibilities for the United States to work to build an effective layered response framework for conflict mitigation in Africa. Through diplomacy, foreign aid, military training, and exchange programs, the United States can contribute to the long-term development of this capacity. Indeed, the 1994 African Conflict Resolution Act (P.L. 103-381) authorizes direct U.S. foreign assistance to the OAU and to subregional organizations to promote conflict management. Within this context, analysts at the symposium suggested a wide range of potential U.S. policy options, such as the following.

- The United States should support the OAU mechanism for conflict prevention, management, and resolution by providing mediation and problem-solving training, organizational training and assistance, and logistics or support for specific missions. U.S. diplomatic efforts should be coordinated to provide both diplomatic and financial or resource assistance support to the OAU and other conflict resolution initiatives when this is desirable.

- The United States should consider supporting the creation of a standing unit of trained administrators—sometimes referred to as "blue hats"—to help with peacemaking and postpeace agreement reconstruction and development.

- The United States should help create an indigenous capacity for humanitarian relief operations by Africans. The United States can assist in this initiative through continued training and by providing pre-positioned material support and targeted development programs—communications equipment, warehouses, transportation infrastructure—to bring such a plan to fruition.

- When appropriate and feasible, the United States should support particularly promising peacekeeping operations on the continent, including UN missions and possible future subregional missions. Support can come in the form of conflict resolution skills training, military equipment, training of soldiers for nontraditional operations, logistics, and communications.

- The United States should provide wide exposure for U.S.-based experts on mediation, problem solving, early warning, and preventive diplomacy through its education and cultural exchange programs.

- Continued support for political liberalization, human rights, and good governance in Africa can help mitigate conflicts in Africa, and power sharing may be an appropriate policy option in the initial phases of transitions. Military and police training may be used to inculcate a respect for human rights and evenhanded policing.

- The United States should directly fund African NGOs working to provide conflict resolution services or research and analysis that can provide early warning or options for ameliorative strategies. Herman Cohen argues, for example, that the United States has "a tendency to want to give aid only to the governmental sector. Let's bypass it. Let's beef up the private sector, but not any old NGO . . . but those who are ready to go in there and jump in and work on conflict and devote themselves to conflict management."

Although all of the above options are realistic and feasible, there are clear constraints to U.S. policy engagement in African conflict management. Analysts are nearly unanimous in their view that the principal constraint is related to the question of political will, or a reluctance to become involved at an earlier stage when involvement is potentially more cost-effective and productive. Constraints that prevent Africans from acting on their own are the very same constraints that may prevent a more engaged U.S. foreign policy with regard to promoting conflict resolution in Africa. Robert Oakley is one who regularly voices concerns about the lack of foresight and sustainability in U.S. policy. He notes with regard to Rwanda, for example, that "with great reluctance, the world was finally moved to carry out a massive humanitarian operation and, yet, now has gone back to sleep and is watching the situation build up where it can very easily explode all over [again]." Oakley's concern is echoed by other former senior policymakers, such as James Woods, who argues that there is a "desire to be detached and to minimize resource inputs. . . . This fatal defect in our system has to be corrected from the top down in order for us to advance on a broad front."

If U.S. policy is to help build a viable institutional conflict response mechanism in Africa—to give meaning to the notion of layered response—long-term commitment is required, which in turn demands both a general consensus on institutional capacity-building in Africa as a critical foreign policy objective as well as adequate supporting resources sustained over a longer period of time. James Woods suggests that "none of this is possible without a reasonable degree of bipartisan agreement on foreign policy issues."

9

CONCLUSION

What Kind of U.S. Role in African Conflict Resolution?

Chester A. Crocker

INTRODUCTION

The preceding chapters discuss how to move toward a strengthened U.S. leadership role in averting, coping with, and resolving African conflicts. While there are differences of emphasis and approach among scholars and practitioners in this field, the era of great ideological schisms is past. We are all awed by the enormity of the challenges facing the leaders and citizens of Africa's externally defined nation-states. Most observers recognize that African conflicts cannot be "blamed" on some convenient scapegoat. The sharp contrast between Africa's relative stability during the Cold War and today is widely understood as the ironic consequence of profound systemic change, both globally and in Africa.

Meanwhile, phrases like "donor fatigue" have come to reflect, however unfairly, external views of everything African. Herman Cohen reminds us that "conflict fatigue" is not far behind. The actual circumstances of African conflict are virtually unknown to the vast majority of American citizens or to their elected representatives until the balloon goes up somewhere, and bloody mayhem breaks out to challenge the humanitarian sentiment of the general public (as focused by the media, NGOs, and advocacy groups). Opinion is unstable, volatile, lacking in memory, and grounded in clichés.

The sharp decline in external enthusiasm for African peacemaking reflects a basic change in western policy orientation and in the nature of African conflicts themselves.

Against such a backdrop, scholars and practitioners find themselves responding to a form of global triage. Lacking apparent concrete and specific national interests in, say, Rwanda, western public opinion can easily be led to accept the logic of post–Cold War disengagement. If Bosnians are left to bleed, why should we act in central Africa? The prevailing opinion seems to be that, lacking comprehensible maps and steady hands on the tiller, our ship of state has crashed on Somalia's shores in an ambitious but misguided attempt to do God's work. It is a sad commentary on the level of our public discourse and on the character of political leadership in both parties and the executive and legislative branches that Somalia—where Americans and our African, European, and Asian partners saved hundreds of thousands of lives—is viewed as a metaphor for foreign policy failure.

The truth, however, is too complex to squeeze into a soundbite. The regrettable result is a tendency to accept as a given that the United States can no longer provide clear and effective leadership in response to African conflicts and crises because it is just not politically feasible. Such a conclusion is valid only if our political leadership takes the short-term view, advocating a disengagement message that they think the voters want to hear. Specialists on African conflict management do no service if, by accepting it, they encourage our national leaders to cop out.

There are many things that specialists and professionals in this field can do, as the preceding chapters make clear. Perhaps the most important is to underscore the variety of options available to help meet the challenge of African conflict and the wide range of things we can responsibly do to strengthen Africa's own capacities. We can also clarify the stages of conflict—in Africa as everywhere else—and the importance of understanding the full life cycle of conflict and the openings available to those who would intervene to help. Too often, public discussion of the challenge of responding to African conflicts focuses narrowly on military intervention by large-scale combat forces, led by the United States within some form of UN context.

Yet that scenario has historically been at the outer fringes of likelihood and feasibility, to say nothing of public popularity. At no time in American history has there been much enthusiasm for direct military involvement in Africa. Indeed, as Africa's conflicts increasingly become complex, internal ethnopolitical struggles, it becomes less likely that outsiders will seek direct military involvement in them. The U.S. political realignment of 1994 and the emergence of a new form of "divided government" only underscores the basic point: It is time to move beyond the "straw man" argument that so often characterizes commentary on African conflicts. Our conclusions should start with the point that there are scores of ways to become involved (or "intervene") in African conflicts apart from direct U.S. combat intervention. Similarly, there may be numerous opportunities for such alternative forms of intervention apart from the moment of looming humanitarian catastrophe, which appears to demand nothing less. All these alternatives represent dramatically lower cost and risk to the intervening actor than the worst case of combat intervention. And, yet, their potential for effectiveness is at least as great as that of the direct application of military coercion. Hence, we should salute those such as Donald Rothchild, Robert Oakley, and Herman Cohen, whose essays illustrate this very point.

LEADERSHIP SHORT OF MILITARY INTERVENTION

There are many forms of external support for conflict resolution in Africa. They range from the preventive or preemptive diplomacy end of the time spectrum to postsettlement participation in friends, observer, or contact groups aimed at keeping an agreement moving forward and on track long after the ink is dry on the initial agreements. We can intervene through traditional bilateral diplomacy; ad hoc coalitions based on a shared interest and commitment to act; indirect diplomacy through support of regional bodies (IGADD or OAU) or key individual states (e.g., the British on Rhodesia-Zimbabwe, Zambia on Angola, Ethiopia on Somalia); economic entities (e.g., the World Bank or the Paris Club), which speak for "the system" (the donors/creditors) and thereby buffer a raw bilateral relationship while bringing real influence to bear; or the passage of UN resolutions when a "universal" voice is considered preferable.

We can intervene with tangible carrots and sticks (e.g., the provision or denial of assistance or trade relations); with the manipulation of symbols conferring or denying legitimacy and standing (visas, invitations, travel policy, public censure, or recognition); and with warnings, promises, advice, coaching, deadlines, threats, hints, conditional offers, side deals, and the quiet understandings and assurances typically associated with confidential diplomacy.

An external party can act on a quick turnaround, ad hoc basis to ward off a negative trend and preempt unhelpful responses by local players. Oakley suggests that American diplomats in Africa do this sort of thing in unheralded ways a dozen times in an average year. One hopes this is an underestimate! But the point is a powerful one: Because of our prestige, intelligence assets, communications capabilities, and widely accepted world order responsibilities we are in a better position than any other government in the world to play this quiet, often effective, and low-cost role of dampening down, forestalling, limiting, and discouraging conflict. If we are not taking such steps a dozen times a year and more, the State Department owes the taxpayers an explanation of why not. This is the classic function of a great power's diplomats in unsettled and unstable areas of the world. The role of U.S. officials in brokering the terms of Meles Zenawi's final takeover in Ethiopia in 1991 is a case in point. On repeated occasions, U.S. and British diplomats quietly supported South Africa's negotiated transition in the early 1990s, a form of sporadic, behind-the-scenes involvement in this negotiation conducted by the local parties themselves.

But there is also the more ambitious category of external leadership in African peacemaking wherein an external power defines and launches (along with appropriate partners) a peace process targeted at a specific zone of conflict, e.g., southern Africa in the 1970s and 1980s. Such mediation efforts demand sustained, high-level commitment to a form of diplomatic engagement that could demand years or even decades of leadership (viz., the Middle East peace process). External actors will not lightly undertake such missions; they are not necessarily costly in material terms, but they can drain energy and political capital on tasks that are seldom popular either at home or in the affected region. Sustained peacemaking places high demands on a nation's reservoir of political will, staying power, strategic intelligence, and what Oakley describes as its capacity for "relentless intensity."

Consequently, in the post–Cold War era, major mediation initiatives will be mounted only when the stakes are comparatively high, the chances for success tolerably good, and the alternatives decidedly grim. Contemporary candidates for such focused intensity of external diplomatic engagement might include Zaire (where there is solid historical precedent for the United States to act in league with our French and Belgian allies); Nigeria for the United States and United Kingdom together; and Sudan for the OAU or a subregional body such as IGADD backed with sustained support from individual African and Arab states, the European Union, and the United States.

The options for intervention can be supported by a wide array of tools and instruments beyond traditional diplomatic and economic pressures and inducements. Clandestine activity remains an instrument of U.S. foreign policy. It might be used where stalemates threaten to break down to the advantage of one side; to preempt a party planning to act in violation of a solemn agreement; or to sabotage and undercut a campaign of Rwandan-style mayhem. Similarly, providing or withholding military assistance to a party engaged in a conflict situation remains a means of direct intervention to move a conflict toward resolution. Such considerations persuaded the British, Portuguese, and others to provide military support to the Mozambican regime before and during the endgame in that country's protracted peace process.

Today more than ever, as Cohen's chapter forcefully illustrates, there may be more valid bases for selective, targeted military assistance to African states and to regional or subregional organizations. Training and equipment can directly support U.S. (and African) interests in (a) civic action; (b) civilian control of the security forces; (c) military downsizing; (d) transitional help with demobilization and retraining in the wake of protracted conflicts; (e) accelerated demining of areas that would otherwise remain lethal to civilian communities; (f) focused peacekeeping training on a regional or subregional basis in coordination with African guidelines and initiatives; and (g) specialized forms of ad hoc military support (humanitarian rescue, logistics, communications) as required to help African forces deployed to deal with African crises.

This inventory is not intended to downplay the importance of Zartman's point that the United States should not be expected to intervene directly in all African preconflict or conflict situations. On the contrary, U.S. intervention will often and increasingly be of the behind-the-scenes coordination, orchestration, and mobilization variety, as he suggests. It would be hard to sustain an argument that the United States should seek to retain its position of the 1980s and early 1990s as Africa's preeminent peacemaker into the indefinite future. But we cannot responsibly disengage from this position by simply refusing to lead when there is no one else to take up the slack. Put another way, it is essential to recognize that even a symbolic U.S. involvement in a multilateral initiative is a crucial inducement and stimulus to others to row on the oars, whereas our absence may trigger the collapse of the whole effort. We ought, therefore, to sustain our leadership, coordinate aggressively with key Europeans and other outsiders who are prepared to participate, and—above all—use our clout to help bring about a broadened burden-sharing in which African governments, private voluntary organizations (PVOs), and regional organizations come to play their proper leading roles.

The bottom line remains an American leadership imperative in African peacemaking. Even the invisible kind can make a crucial difference. Compare the unconscionable delays in fielding an upgraded United Nations Mission in Rwanda (MINUAR) peacekeeping operation in Rwanda after the 1994 massacre began with the fielding in a matter of days of the ONUC operation in the Congo (now Zaire) in 1960! In the latter case, U.S. determination and military logistic assets made things happen (though no U.S. troops were deployed), whereas we rejected the burdens of multilateral leadership in Rwanda, reversing ground only when the French intervened months after the tragedy began.

Can such political will on behalf of African peacemaking be restored to its proper place in U.S. foreign policy? I believe so, after an initial shakedown flowing from the 1994 political realignment. But there are two preconditions. First, our leaders need to find the candor (and a minimum degree of bipartisanship) to lower expectations for such foreign endeavors. Rothchild projects that the results of U.S. mediation efforts will be mixed. That is a safe call, but one worth making to transform the ground rules and revise the standards of measurement applied to U.S. foreign policy. In a more realistic climate of public and media discourse, we would count setbacks in African conflict resolution as normal, the avoidance of defeat as victory, and the achievement of a settlement as a major triumph. Yes, there will be setbacks! And it is high time our public and elected officials found the backbone to say so to media representatives screaming for soundbites.

Second, in discussing African conflicts, U.S. officials need to find a clearer and more concrete voice in articulating to American audiences what is really at stake. For leaders of any major political party to assert that we have no national interests in Africa is to apply an extraordinarily narrow vision of U.S. interests, one that poses dangers down the road. In reality, a number of significant American interests are on the line in Africa. Success in African conflict resolution means a more decent and stable world order, increased exports, and jobs and investment opportunities for Americans. Failure threatens our values and our budgets since eventually we will wind up paying for continuous peacekeeping operations and emergency famine relief programs. It also creates ideal conditions for expanded drug trafficking and state-sponsored terrorism, and fosters ever-growing refugee and migration flows. Failure in Africa means—at some level and at some point—a threat to world health and environmental security. But unless these points are made credibly and forcefully, escapists will continue to reject U.S. leadership, arguing that we can fence off Africa like a strategic slum.

STRENGTHENING AFRICAN CONFLICT RESOLUTION CAPABILITIES

African institution-building and capability enhancement for peacemaking have emerged as common themes in these discussion. Rather than repeat what Zartman, Cohen, and Sisk have said above, it may be useful to summarize the categories of activity under consideration. First, there is the question of enhanced African institutional and organizational capacity for peacemaking, i.e., coherent, purposeful diplomatic intervention in preconflict or conflict scenarios. In response to the initiative of Nigeria's former head of state General Olusegun Obasanjo and other former African leaders—and at the urging of several key western states that offered funding to support greater OAU focus on conflict resolution—the OAU created in 1993 a conflict management mechanism within its secretariat. Despite the enthusiastic backing of donors and of Secretary-General Salim Salim, the mechanism has been slow to become a functional reality because of organizational, personnel, and other problems of "absorptive capacity."

Salim envisages a self-contained unit reporting to him, with a capacity for research and information gathering, policy planning, and coordination of military peacekeeping efforts. It would be supported by specially earmarked units of African security forces. The principle of OAU intervention into the previously forbidden domain of internal affairs has been accepted. In recent years the United States has contributed by providing modest assistance to the OAU itself, backed by training and offers of loaned expertise as requested. Such a policy stance represents both a challenge to member governments to permit greater secretariat authority and a pledge that we can be counted on to support the empowerment of their own peacemakers.

Among the OAU's institutional problems are the suspicions of member governments about an activist secretary-general who wants to change things. But in practice, the OAU, just like the UN, depends on its members, so when nonmembers, like the United States, transfer resources and skills to the regional body, it should be done with some sensitivity for African political realities. For the foreseeable future, in any event, the OAU's sphere of effectiveness will be sharply constrained by such realities. It will need to delegate or defer certain activities to key individual states and leaders or to subregional organizations such as SADC or IGADD. These organizations may be better organized or placed to act as the OAU's agents by engaging in factfinding and observer missions, mediation efforts, and other diplomatic variations of peacemaking. By the same token, the OAU's military role will likely remain derivative, confined to the important but secondary task of contacting troop contributors, coordinating their offers, and supporting their requests for external logistic or equipment aid.

In sum, the assets available in Africa itself are real but finite. In our attempts to strengthen African capacities, we would do well to encourage the OAU and individual governments to take the lead and make better, more efficient use of existing assets. The 1994 Africa Conflict Resolution Act makes an important contribution within this context by channeling modest funds to the OAU and to the purposes of military demobilization. High-profile trips to Africa by senior U.S. officials to underscore U.S. hopes for African leadership in peacemaking also send a message. But we must not imagine that hortatory statements and contributions of a few million dollars to OAU headquarters in Addis Ababa will somehow transform Africa's capabilities and solve the problem. Africa's real peacemaking strengths lie in the presence of scores of highly experienced diplomats and a significant number of veteran African peacemakers as well as administrators in such fields as refugee assistance and public health. Quality people like this—the crucial ingredient of peacemaking—are scattered among Africa's many diplomatic and public service establishments as well as in PVOs and overseas. An inventory of such all-stars who could network with non-African counterparts (as Zartman proposes) would be very useful. This "force in being" would be at the disposal of the OAU or other bodies.

In the meantime, as specific contingencies arise, American diplomats should coordinate closely with allied counterparts to send a coherent signal to Addis Ababa of what we will (and will not) support in each case. The appalling delays in fielding a revised UN force of largely African peacekeepers to Rwanda in the middle of 1994 owe much to an unacceptable confusion among western allies, between them and New York, and among African troop contributors and OAU officials and western nations asked to support their deployment. No side covered itself with glory in this episode. When so many actors are involved and no one wants sole responsibility for a "mediagenic" humanitarian crisis, it is predictable that confusion and disorganization will prolong the agony. But the point is that U.S. diplomatic leadership should have been exerted at whatever level was required to isolate the problems and resolve them.

THE VITAL IMPORTANCE OF IMPLEMENTATION

Experience on the ground confirms the results of cutting-edge research at the United States Institute of Peace (USIP) and elsewhere: Effective, hands-on support for implementation of settlements and agreements is as important as any other phase of peacemaking. The agony of Angola bears continuing witness to the importance of thinking in advance about how a settlement can be implemented, how to ensure that it does not become "orphaned" (in the words of USIP fellow Fen Hampson) by its original sponsors, and how to ensure that adequate resources will be made available for successful implementation.

Very few peace agreements are self-executing, and most cannot be viewed as static documents engraved in stone. They require continuous and creative adaptation in light of changing conditions on the ground and the evolving chemistry between former adversaries. When a settlement aims to transform relationships and fundamentally alter the way people pursue their political goals, it is essential that it have the sustained backing of the external, non-African community to channel ideas, resources, models, and know-how to the local actors. No area of African peacemaking is in greater need of tangible support than the field of demilitarization, demobilization, disarmament, and demining. These are vital elements of transition assistance, which are only now beginning to receive appropriate support from the United States and other powers.

But the transition to a civil order will require more than resources. Leadership and a strong hand are sometimes required to keep former warring parties from blowing up fragile accords. Typically, that strong hand will be an external one: a special representative of the UN or OAU secretary-general, or a friends or contact group of governments interested in the peace process. External leadership is required to broker compromises; shame and show up violators and bad actors; bring moral and other suasion to bear if required; legitimize fresh compromises; and generally to call meetings, set deadlines, and create a continuous flow of pressures to keep the peace train on track.

There are a few guidebooks on these matters, and it is perhaps best to conclude with comments that underscore the unique aspects of each case. In Mozambique's transition, the UN special representative Aldo Ajello played a masterful role. His personal qualities and implicit backing from Rome—the patron capital and site of the Mozambique peace process—helped to overcome the worse-than-normal inadequacies of the UN bureaucratic system as well as the often obtuse and uncooperative conduct of the parties. Ajello's role is a metaphor for Mozambique's likely prolonged reliance on outside help to get back on its feet after more than thirty years of turmoil. Given the Italian official and PVO leadership role in Mozambique, Washington has not been required to play a high-profile role as a patron of the settlement process, yet U.S. involvement has been important at every stage. And, at critical junctures, the public and private words of American diplomats have made a decisive difference in moderating the behavior of the parties.

In other circumstances, implementation has been deemed so important that it should be institutionalized. The 1988 Angola-Namibia settlement provided for a joint commission linking the three signatory nations (Angola, Cuba, and South Africa) and the United States and USSR as "observers" with the ad hoc participation of UN officials. The joint commission met bimonthly for most of the twenty-seven-month implementation period, providing institutional underpinning for the agreements in the form of an instantly available court of first appeal in the event of trouble. The commission saved the settlement on at least one occasion.

The point, of course, is that effective implementation of peace agreements—like the earlier phases of the peacemaking process—demands leadership and a willingness to engage. The costs of committed participation may be lower, in the long run, than the costs of opting out or simply going along for the ride.

TOWARD AN AFRICAN REGIONAL ORDER

As African leaders and their friends from other countries consider the post–Cold War legacy facing the region, some basic choices of orientation impose themselves. If we are to focus our attention on preventive action, we will have to identify some criteria and categories for recognizing dangerous situations. Already, we are faced with half a dozen collapsed or collapsing states. Ali Mazrui and Bethuel Kiplagat have suggested criteria for spotting trouble. One of the clearest is Mazrui's dual society, in which there is "pure ethnic differentiation without territorial differentiation." In practice, this means that Rwanda and Burundi may be the most dangerously conflict-prone societies in Africa, now that South Africa is postapartheid. These two countries have more in common with Northern Ireland and Bosnia than with, say, Liberia or Somalia. Kiplagat's criteria point to a far longer list of potentially threatened African societies, but at a lower and more generalized threat level. This takes us back to Zartman's point that there is no shortage of warnings and telltale signs: The challenge is knowing which ones to take seriously and how to organize the response.

It is surely correct to argue, as most contributors to this volume do, that African regional order will depend in the long run on clearly articulated norms and guidelines supporting improved governance, democratization, and respect for the rights of minorities. Support for these objectives can, therefore, be viewed as integral to a conflict resolution strategy. But desired results do not follow automatically from sanctions, sermons, aid cutoffs, and other such measures for expressing our displeasure with Africa's autocrats. Nor are they likely to occur once the spiral of collapse has begun.

So the question is, what specifically can be done to avert the threat of incipient government collapse and strengthen the capacity to govern? It is important to recall once again that recent African disorders are the result of government weakness, not tyranny. This creates a dilemma for western nations and donors as they decide how to tailor their assistance to individual countries whose records on all the western desiderata may be mixed, but whose governments may look much better than the alternatives. Sustained, focused, and timely assistance to threatened societies has to be an element of a wise preventive diplomacy. Thus one wonders at the spasmodic behavior of western donors who throw everything in sight into Rwandan refugee camps to save lives but appear paralyzed with uncertainty about whether to assist the new Rwandan government despite its commitments to reconciliation and justice.

In the end, it is hard to escape the conclusion that African conflict resolution in all its forms will be more successful if the region's linkages with the external world are progressively strengthened. It is easy enough to look at the least successful parts of this crisis-torn continent and recoil in alarm or distaste. It is also easy to punish, isolate, criticize, sanction, and shun African miscreants—in some cases bringing an end to current forms of misrule and abuse. The hard part, however, is to create successes and make things better. This, of course, is a task for Africans. But they will need an engaged western world at their sides.

NOTES

CHAPTER 1. SMOCK, "INTRODUCTION"

1. Jennifer Parmelee, "Africans Told To Expect Less from the U.S.," *Washington Post,* December 16, 1994.

2. R. Jeffrey Smith, "Demand for Humanitarian Aid May Skyrocket," *Washington Post,* December 17, 1994, p. A22.

3. "Africa: Unmaking and Remaking the State," *Africa Confidential* 36, no. 1 (January 6, 1995):1–4.

4. Herman Cohen, "Getting Rwanda Wrong," *New York Times,* June 3, 1994, p. A23.

5. Roger Winter, "Journey into Genocide: A Rwanda Diary," *Washington Post,* June 5, 1994, p. C1.

6. James Gustave Speth, "Africa: Conflict Prevention and New Development Initiatives," unpublished paper presented at the African-American Institute, New York, May 24, 1994.

7. "Statement by the Secretary General H. E. Salim Ahmed Salim at the White House Conference on Africa," State Department, Washington, D.C., June 26, 1994.

8. Howard W. French, "U.S. Diplomatic Mission on 5-Nation Africa Tour," *New York Times,* October 24, 1994, p. A6.

9. William Drozdiak, "France Urges Africa to Form Peacekeeping Force," *Washington Post,* November 10, 1994, p. A54.

10. Olusegun Obasanjo and Felix G. N. Mosha, eds., *Africa: Rise to the Challenge: Towards a Conference on Security, Stability, Development and Cooperation in Africa* (New York: Africa Leadership Forum, 1993).

11. This book has benefited significantly from the very helpful editorial suggestions offered by Guy Martin and James Woods.

CHAPTER 2. MAZRUI, "THE AFRICAN STATE AS A POLITICAL REFUGEE"

1. Based on a paper originally presented at the symposium in Addis Ababa, Ethiopia, sponsored by the OAU and the UN High Commissioner for Refugees, September 5–7, 1994. An earlier and shorter version was presented in Cairo at the consultation "The OAU Mechanism on Conflict Prevention, Management, and Resolution," sponsored by the OAU, the International Peace Academy, and the government of Egypt, May 2–7, 1994.

2. See, for example, Robert H. Jackson and Carl G. Rosberg, "Why Africa's Weak States Persist: The Empirical and the Juridical in Statehood," in *The State and Development in the Third World*, edited by Atul Kohli (Princeton, N.J.: Princeton University Press, 1986), pp. 259–82.

3. See "South Africa: Sharing Power," *Africa Confidential* 35, no. 10 (May 20, 1994):1–5; "South Africa: The Mandate for Mandela," *Africa Confidential* 35, no. 9 (May 6, 1994):1–5.

4. See, for example, Naomi Chazan et al., *Politics and Society in Contemporary Africa* (Boulder: Lynne Rienner, 1988), especially pp. 101–25.

5. See for example, Arthur S. Banks, ed., *Political Handbook of the World 1993* (Binghamton, N.Y.: CSA Publications, 1994), pp. 211–16, 735–38.

6. See, for example, Dunstan M. Wai, *The African-Arab Conflict in the Sudan* (New York: Africana Publishing, 1981); M. O. Beshir, *The Southern Sudan: Background to Conflict* (New York: Hurst, 1968).

7. This was a quotation from a Christian missionary who witnessed the carnage in the central African country that *Time* decided to use over a picture of a Rwandan mother holding her baby at a refugee camp near Ngara, Tanzania. See *Time*, May 16, 1994, cover page and pp. 56–63. See also "Rwanda: Civilian Slaughter," *Africa Confidential* 35, no. 9 (May 6, 1994):5–6; "Rwanda: A Double Agenda," *Africa Confidential* 35, no. 10 (May 20, 1994):8; "Rwanda: From Coup to Carnage," *Africa Confidential* 35, no. 8 (April 15, 1994):8; "Streets of Slaughter," *Time*, April 25, 1994, pp. 45–46; "Rwanda: All the Hatred in the World," *Time*, June 13, 1994, pp. 36–37.

8. See Ali A. Mazrui, "Social Engineering and Political Bridge-Building for the 21st Century: An African Agenda," keynote address at a youth conference, "Nigeria in the 21st Century," sponsored by the Yakubu Gowon Centre for the Promotion of National Unity and International Cooperation, Abuja, Nigeria, September 14–16, 1994.

9. For example, on June 9, 1994, the RPF announced that the Roman Catholic archbishop of Kigali and several other priests had been murdered by four of its own troops and that the RPF would see to it that the perpetrators were brought to justice.

CHAPTER 4. ROTHCHILD, "THE U.S. ROLE IN MANAGING AFRICAN CONFLICTS: LESSONS FROM THE PAST"

1. Parts of this paper are drawn from my chapter, "The United States and Conflict Management in Africa," in *Africa in World Politics*, edited by John Harbeson and Donald Rothchild, 2d ed. (Boulder: Westview, 1995), chap. 10.

2. Stephen John Stedman, *Peacemaking in Civil Wars: International Mediation in Zimbabwe, 1974–1980* (Boulder: Lynne Rienner, 1990), pp. 5–9.

3. Highlighting the intensity of civil wars, Paul Pillar's data indicate that nearly twice as many interstate wars ended with negotiations as did civil wars. See Paul R. Pillar, *Negotiating Peace: War Termination as a Bargaining Process* (Princeton, N.J.: Princeton University Press, 1983), pp. 5–7.

4. Senate Resolution 94, *Congressional Record—Senate* 139, no. 46 (April 3, 1993): S4508; House Concurrent Resolution 131, 103d Cong., 1st sess. (August 3, 1993):5–6.

5. "Kenya: A Difficult Courtship," *Africa Confidential* 34, no. 20 (October 8, 1993):4.

6. See Donald Rothchild and Caroline Hartzell, "The Case of Angola: Four Power Intervention and Disengagement," in *Foreign Military Intervention*, edited by Ariel E. Levite, Bruce W. Jentleson, and Larry Berman (New York: Columbia University Press, 1992), pp. 163–207.

7. Eddie Becker and Christopher Mitchell, *Chronology of Conflict Resolution Initiatives in Sudan* (Fairfax, Va.: George Mason University, Institute for Conflict Analysis and Resolution, 1991), pp. 111–12.

8. Bona Malwal, "Breathing New Life into the American Initiative?" *Sudan Democratic Gazette*, no. 14 (July 1991):4–5.

9. Gillian Gunn, "A Guide to the Intricacies of the Angola-Namibia Negotiations," *CSIS Africa Notes*, no. 90 (September 8, 1988):12.

10. Rothchild and Hartzell, "The Case of Angola," p. 185; Michael McFaul, "The Demise of the World Revolutionary Process: Soviet-Angolan Relations under Gorbachev," *Journal of Southern African Studies* 16 (1990):182–83.

11. Chester A. Crocker, *High Noon in Southern Africa: Making Peace in a Rough Neighborhood* (New York: Norton, 1992), p. 397.

12. Raymond W. Copson and Theodros S. Dagne, *Somalia: Operation Restore Hope* (Washington, D.C.: Congressional Research Service, 1993), p. 1.

13. See Hussein M. Adam, "Somalia: Militarism, Warlordism, or Democracy?" *Review of African Political Economy*, no. 54 (1992):18; Rakiya Omaar, "Somalia: At War with Itself," *Current History* 91, no. 565 (May 1992):233.

14. John Garang de Mabior, *Appeal to the Sudanese People on the Founding of the Sudan People's Liberation Army (SPLA) and Sudan People's Liberation Movement (SPLM)* (Sudan: SPLM/SPLA, 1984), p. 5.

15. Holly J. Burkhalter, "The Question of Genocide: The Clinton Administration and Rwanda," *World Policy Journal* 11, no. 4 (winter 1994/95):53.

16. Adam Przeworski, *Democracy and the Market* (Cambridge, England: Cambridge University Press, 1991), pp. 14, 29.

17. Tony Lake, "Remarks," delivered at the Brookings Africa Forum Luncheon, May 3, 1993.

18. Daniel Brumberg, "Some Thoughts on Fundamentalist Utopias and the Question of Democratic Transitions," paper delivered at the Conference on Regime Change and Democratization in Comparative Perspective, University of California, Los Angeles, May 19–21, 1994, p. 11.

19. John Gerald Ruggie, "The U.N.: Between Peacekeeping and Enforcement," *Foreign Affairs: Agenda 1994* (New York: Foreign Affairs, 1994), p. 99.

CHAPTER 5. OAKLEY, "A DIPLOMATIC PERSPECTIVE ON AFRICAN CONFLICT RESOLUTION"

1. Brian Urquhart, *Ralph Bunche: An American Life* (New York: Norton, 1993), p. 334.

CHAPTER 6. COHEN, "AFRICAN CAPABILITIES FOR MANAGING CONFLICT: THE ROLE OF THE UNITED STATES"

1. See OAU documents: *Report of the Secretary-General on Conflicts in Africa: Proposals for an OAU Mechanism for Conflict Prevention and Resolution*, Dakar, Senegal, June 1992; *Interim Report of the Secretary-General on the Mechanism for Conflict Prevention, Management and Resolution*, Addis Ababa, Ethiopia, February 1993.

2. While non-Africans provided the leadership in addressing internal conflict during the 1987–93 period, African governments and eminent persons were not absent. For example, President Moi and Permanent Secretary Kiplagat of Kenya performed important services in the Mozambique negotiations. Presidents Mobutu of Zaire, Sassou-Nguessou of the Congo, Bongo of Gabon, and Pereira of Cape Verde at various times did important work in the Angolan conflict. In Liberia, of course, Africans were the leaders and have done most of the work.

3. When the ECOWAS intervention in Liberia led by Nigeria took place in mid-1990, the OAU secretary-general was called in after the fact and was asked to provide OAU endorsement of the operation, which he did. By contrast, when the president and most of the Burundi ministers were murdered in 1992 in a botched military coup, Salim felt free to jump right in and begin negotiating the introduction of an OAU monitoring group.

4. The best example of this phenomenon in 1994 has been the negotiations on the southern Sudan war being mediated by IGADD, which groups together the countries of the Horn of Africa. Although both the Sudanese government and the southern insurgents of the Sudan People's Liberation Army have had good tactical reasons not to negotiate, they have faithfully turned up at IGADD negotiating sessions because of this OAU peer pressure.

5. For an analysis of the OAU's Chad mediation effort, see Samuel G. Amoo, "Frustrations of Regional Peacekeeping: The OAU in Chad, 1977–1982," mimeographed paper, prepared under the auspices of the Institute of Conflict Analysis and Resolution, George Mason University. There appears to be no published account of the short-lived Angola negotiations led by Mobutu of Zaire in 1989, but the author was involved on a day-to-day basis.

6. Samuel G. Amoo, "The OAU and African Conflicts: The Political and Institutional Dynamics of Regional Conflict Management," Ph.D. dissertation, Johns Hopkins University, 1989; Francis Deng and I. William Zartman, eds., *Conflict Resolution in Africa* (Washington, D.C.: Brookings Institution, 1991); Virginia Page Fortuna, *Regional Organizations and Peacekeeping*, Occasional Paper No. 11 (Washington, D.C.: Henry L. Stimson Center, 1993).

7. It is only fair to point out that African reticence about getting involved in internal conflict was a reflection as much of the international community's attitude as of the OAU doctrine of noninterference in internal affairs. Apart from the Congo in 1960, which was a collapsed state, there was very little multilateral intervention in internal conflict until the great wave started with UNAVEM in Angola in 1989.

8. Fortuna, *Regional Organizations and Peacekeeping*, pp. 28–30.

9. In popular parlance, "peacekeeping" has become an all-encompassing term covering all military operations in support of conflict management. Whenever military intervenors have to engage in fighting, therefore, the mission is automatically deemed a failure. The author remembers that when ECOMOG was fighting the NPFL rebels in Liberia, a number of senior U.S. officials described the situation by saying, "ECOMOG is now part of the problem." Peacekeeping, of course, is just one of several possible mandates. It means monitoring and observing in an effort to maintain a cease-fire or uphold a peace agreement so that those involved do not attempt to cheat. In such cases, the outbreak of fighting terminates the mission. Peace enforcement, on the other hand, involves a combat mandate in which the military units will be prepared to use force to accomplish their mission, usually under chapter VII of the UN charter.

10. The United States provided $27 million in nonlethal aid to ECOMOG via ECOWAS, and an additional $15 million to Senegal to help transport and equip the battalion it deployed to Liberia in 1991. Accurate data on the cost to ECO-MOG contributors are not available, but Nigeria alone is estimated to have spent several hundred million dollars to maintain its troops in Liberia.

11. The ECOMOG experience demonstrates the dangers of a subregional operation where there may not be a formal mandate backed up by a clear time frame for withdrawal and a funded budget. Delays in negotiations and even more delays in implementing agreements have unfortunately made the ECOWAS sojourn in Liberia quasi-permanent.

12. Thomas L. Friedman, "Bush Address to the UN Urges More Vigor in Peacekeeping," *New York Times*, September 22, 1992, p. 1.

13. Herman J. Cohen, "Intervention in Somalia," in *The Diplomatic Record 1992–1993* (Boulder: Westview, 1994), pp. 51–80.

14. Department of State, *The Clinton Administration's Policy on Reforming Multilateral Peace Operations,* Washington, D.C.: Bureau of International Organization Affairs, 1994.

15. Barry M. Blechman and J. Matthew Vaccaro, *Training for Peace-Keeping: The United Nations' Role,* Report No. 12 (Washington, D.C.: Henry L. Stimson Center, 1994). A small pilot program for UN training for peacekeeping, proposed in this publication, is being funded by the Ford Foundation.

16. Heads of State and Government of the OAU, Twenty-ninth Ordinary Session in Cairo, June 28–30, 1993, Declaration AHG/DECL.3 (XXIX) Rev.1.

17. Salim Ahmed Salim, secretary-general of the OAU, speech to the White House Conference on Africa, dinner hosted by Secretary of State Warren Christopher, June 26, 1994. See excerpts in *CSIS Africa Notes,* no. 162.

18. African Conflict Resolution Act, HR-4541 of 1994.

19. Blechman and Vaccaro, *Training for Peace-Keeping.*

20. As reported by representatives of the Global Coalition for Africa who were present for the sessions in Tunis.

21. The Subcommittee on Democracy and Governance of the Global Coalition for Africa has proposed that such a network be constituted under the name Africa Reconciliation. See "An OAU-GCA Initiative on Preventive Diplomacy in Africa," available from the Global Coalition for Africa, 1850 K Street, NW, Suite 295, Washington, DC 20006.

22. Such a project is elaborated in "Africa and the United Nations Agenda for Peace: A Proposal," available from the Global Coalition for Africa, 1850 K Street, NW, Suite 295, Washington, DC 20006.

23. Department of State, *Clinton Administration's Policy.*

24. American diplomatic mission personnel, from all agencies, should be trained to observe and report on those elements of civil security that are likely to lead to insecurity, conflict, and violence. This goes beyond the standard reporting on human rights. The issues include power sharing, fairness to all ethnic groups and regions, revenue sharing, good governance, and corruption. The United States should make efforts to have a dialogue with governments on these subjects to seek corrective action that would preempt conflict. Indeed, as an addendum to the annual Human Rights Report, there might be a section entitled "Precursors of Conflict."

25. The role model for the settlement of conflict through nonviolent means is probably Belgium, where the Walloons and the Flemish could not have more acrimonious arguments over the division of power and resources, yet they manage to avoid violence.

CHAPTER 8. SISK, "INSTITUTIONAL CAPACITY-BUILDING FOR AFRICAN CONFLICT MANAGEMENT: SUMMARY OF THE DISCUSSION"

1. Throughout this essay, unless otherwise noted, quotations are remarks made at the United States Institute of Peace symposium "The U.S. Role in Conflict Prevention, Management, and Resolution in Africa," September 28, 1994.

2. See Michael Lund, *Preventive Diplomacy: A Strategy for Preventing Violent Conflicts* (Washington, D.C.: United States Institute of Peace Press, forthcoming).

3. Olara Otunnu argues that such a community of values is "conspicuously missing" in Africa—for example, on fundamental issues such as the maintenance of democracy or the protection of human rights. Mazrui, on the other hand, contends that the values are there; what is lacking is the political will to implement them.

4. Robert A. Mortimer, "ECOMOG, Liberia, and Regional Security in West Africa," in *The End of the Cold War and the New African Political Order,* edited by Edmond Keller and Donald Rothchild (forthcoming).

5. For further details on the IGADD process and ways the international community can enhance the prospects for a negotiated settlement, see the United States Institute of Peace Special Report *Sudan: Ending the War, Moving Talks Forward* (May 1994). For information on earlier peacemaking initiatives, see the Special Report *Sudan Symposium Generates Momentum for Mediation* (October 1993).

6. For recent academic analysis of transitions in Africa, see Michael Bratton and Nicolas van de Walle, "Neopatrimonial Regimes and Political Transitions in Africa," *World Politics* 46, no. 4 (July 1994):453–89.

7. For a detailed account of the South African experience, see Timothy D. Sisk, *Democratization in South Africa: The Elusive Social Contract* (Princeton, N.J.: Princeton University Press, 1995).

8. See the World Bank Discussion Paper "Demobilization and Reintegration of Military Personnel in Africa: The Evidence from Seven Case Studies," Report IDP-130, which places considerable emphasis on NGO-based programs.

9. For further details on the South African experience, including the role of the UN and OAU in the transition process, see Peter Gastrow, *Bargaining for Peace: South Africa and the National Peace Accord* (Washington, D.C.: United States Institute of Peace Press, 1995); Timothy D. Sisk, "South Africa's National Peace Accord," *Peace & Change* 19, no. 1 (January 1994):50–70; United States Institute of Peace Special Report, *South Africa: The National Peace Accord and the International Community* (September 1993).

ABBREVIATIONS

AACC	All-Africa Conference of Churches
AAS	African Academy of Sciences
ANC	African National Congress (South Africa)
ANC	*Armée Nationale Congolaise*
CEAO	West African Economic Community (for franco-phone states) *(Communauté Economique de l'Afrique de l'Ouest)*
CSSDCA	Conference on Security, Stability, Development, and Cooperation in Africa
DHA	Department of Humanitarian Affairs (United Nations)
ECOMOG	ECOWAS Monitoring Group (emergency force in Liberia)
ECOWAS	Economic Community of West African States
EPLF	Eritrean People's Liberation Front
EPRDF	Ethiopian People's Revolutionary Democratic Front
FAR	*Forces Armées Rwandaises*
FNLA	Angolan National Liberation Front *(Front National de Liberation de l'Angola)*
FPR	*Front Patriotique Rwandais*
GCA	Global Coalition for Africa
IBRD	International Bank for Reconstruction and Development (World Bank)
ICRC	International Committee of the Red Cross
IGADD	Intergovernmental Authority on Drought and Development

IMF	International Monetary Fund
MINUAR	United Nations Mission in Rwanda
MPLA	Popular Movement for the Liberation of Angola *(Movimento Popular de Libertacao de Angola)*
NGO	nongovernmental organization
NORDSAMFN	Joint Nordic Committee for United Nations Military Matters
NPFL	National Patriotic Front of Liberia
OAU	Organization of African Unity
ONUC	United Nations organization in the Congo
PDD	Presidential Decision Directive
RENAMO	Mozambique National Resistance *(Resistencia Nacional Mocambicana)*
RPF	Rwanda Patriotic Front
SADC	Southern African Development Community
SADF	South African Defense Force
SNA	Somali National Alliance
SPLA	Sudan People's Liberation Army
SPLM	Sudan People's Liberation Movement
SRO	subregional organization
SWAPO	South West Africa People's Organization
UNAMIR	United Nations Assistance in Rwanda
UNAVEM	United Nations Angola Verification Mission
UNDP	United Nations Development Program
UNHCR	United Nations High Commissioner for Refugees
UNICEF	United Nations Children's Fund
UNITA	National Union for the Total Independence of Angola *(Uniao Nacional para a Indepencia Total de Angola)*
UNITAF	United Task Force (U.S.-led multinational force deployed in Somalia, December 1992)
UNTAG	United Nations Transition Assistance Group (Namibia)
USAID	United States Agency for International Development
USIA	United States Information Agency
WFP	World Food Program
ZAPU	Zimbabwe African People's Union

FURTHER READING

Adam, Hussein M. "Somalia: Militarism, Warlordism, or Democracy?" *Review of African Political Economy* 54 (1992): 18–26.

Ake, Claude. "Rethinking African Democracy." *Journal of Democracy* 2 (1991): 33–44.

Amoo, Samuel G. "The OAU and African Conflicts: The Political and Institutional Dynamics of Regional Conflict Management." Ph.D. dissertation, Johns Hopkins University, 1989.

Amoo, Samuel G., and I. William Zartman. "Mediation by Regional Organizations: The Organization of African Unity (OAU) in Chad," in *Mediation in International Relations,* edited by Jacob Bercovitch and Jeffrey Rubin (New York: St. Martin's, 1992).

Arnold, Millard. "Engaging South Africa after Apartheid." *Foreign Policy* 87 (1992): 139–56.

Baker, Pauline H. *The United States and South Africa: The Reagan Years.* New York: Ford Foundation, 1989.

Boutros-Ghali, Boutros. *An Agenda for Peace.* New York: United Nations, 1992.

Bratton, Michael, and Nicolas van de Walle. "Neopatrimonial Regimes and Political Transitions in Africa." *World Politics* 46, no. 4 (July 1994): 453–89.

Clough, Michael. *Free at Last? U.S. Policy toward Africa and the End of the Cold War.* New York: Council on Foreign Relations, 1992.

Cohen, Herman J. "Intervention in Somalia," in *The Diplomatic Record 1992–1993.* Boulder: Westview, 1994.

Crocker, Chester. *High Noon in Southern Africa: Making Peace in a Rough Neighborhood.* New York: Norton, 1992.

Davidson, Basil. *The Black Man's Burden: Africa and the Curse of the Nation-State.* New York: Times Books, 1992.

Deng, Francis. "Africa and the New World Dis-Order: Rethinking Colonial Boundaries." *Brookings Review* 11, no. 2 (1993): 32–35.

Deng, Francis, and A. A. An-Na´im, eds. *Human Rights in Africa: Cross-Cultural Perspectives.* Washington, D.C.: Brookings Institution, 1990.

Deng, Francis, and I. William Zartman, eds. *Conflict Resolution in Africa.* Washington, D.C.: Brookings Institution, 1991.

Deng, Francis, I. William Zartman, Sadikiel Kimaro, Terrence P. Lyons, and Donald Rothchild. *Sovereignty as Responsibility: Conflict Resolution in Africa.* Washington, D.C.: Brookings Institution, forthcoming.

Fortuna, Virginia Page. *Regional Organizations and Peacekeeping.* Occasional Paper No. 11. Washington, D.C.: Henry L. Stimson Center, 1993.

Gastrow, Peter. *Bargaining for Peace: South Africa and the National Peace Accord.* Washington, D.C.: United States Institute of Peace Press, 1995.

Gibbs, Richard N. *The Political Economy of Third World Intervention: Mines, Money, and U.S. Policy in the Congo Crisis.* Chicago: University of Chicago Press, 1991.

Glickman, Harvey, ed. *Toward Peace and Security in Southern Africa.* New York: Gordon and Breach, 1990.

Hume, Cameron. *Ending Mozambique's War: The Role of Mediation and Good Offices.* Washington, D.C.: United States Institute of Peace Press, 1994.

Hyden, Goran, and Michael Bratton, eds. *Governance and Politics in Africa.* Boulder: Lynne Rienner, 1992.

Jabri, Vivienne. *Mediating Conflict: Decision-Making and Western Intervention in Namibia.* Manchester, UK: Manchester University Press, 1990.

Jaster, Robert S., Moeletsi Mbeki, Morley Nkosi, and Michael Clough, eds. *Changing Fortunes: War, Diplomacy, and Economics in Southern Africa.* New York: Ford Foundation/Foreign Policy Association, 1992.

Jonah, James. "The OAU: Peacekeeping and Conflict Resolution," in *The OAU after 30 Years,* edited by Yassin El-Ayouty. New York: Praeger, 1994.

Joseph, Richard. "The Clinton Administration and Africa: The Democratic Imperative." *Africa Demos* 3, no. 3 (September 1994): 12–19.

Khadiagala, Gilbert M., and Hizkias Assefa. *Conflict and Conflict Resolution in the Horn of Africa.* Washington, D.C.: Brookings Institution, forthcoming.

Laidi, Zaki. *The Superpowers and Africa: The Constraints of a Rivalry, 1960–1990.* Chicago: University of Chicago Press, 1990.

Lemarchand, René. *Burundi: Ethnocide as Discourse and Practice.* Washington, D.C.: Woodrow Wilson Center Press/Cambridge University Press, 1994.

Lulat, Y. G. M. *U.S. Relations with South Africa: An Annotated Bibliography.* Boulder: Westview, 1991.

Lund, Michael. *Preventive Diplomacy: A Strategy for Preventing Violent Conflicts.* Washington, D.C.: United States Institute of Peace Press, forthcoming.

Maluwa, Tiyanjana. "The Peaceful Settlement of Disputes among African States, 1963–1983: Some Conceptual Issues and Practical Trends." *International and Comparative Law Quarterly* 35, no. 3 (1989): 299–320.

Mazrui, Ali. "Africa: In Search of Self-Pacification." *African Affairs* 93, no. 2 (1994): 39–42.

Mortimer, Robert A. "ECOMOG, Liberia, and Regional Security in West Africa," in *The End of the Cold War and the New African Political Order,* edited by Edmond Keller and Donald Rothchild, forthcoming.

Newbury, Catherine. "Introduction: Paradoxes of Democratization in Africa." *African Studes Review* 37, no. 1 (April 1994): 1–8.

Obasanjo, Olusegun, and Felix G. N. Mosha, eds. *Africa: Rise to the Challenge: Towards a Conference on Security, Stability, Development, and Cooperation in Africa.* New York: Africa Leadership Forum, 1993.

Ohlson, Thomas, Stephen John Stedman, and Robert Davies. *The New Is Not Yet Born: Conflict Resolution in Southern Africa.* Washington, D.C.: Brookings Institution, 1994.

Organization of African Unity. *Resolving Conflicts in Africa: Implementation Options.* OAU Information Services Publication, Series II. Addis Ababa, Ethiopia: Organization of African Unity, 1993.

Robinson, Pearl. "Democratization: Understanding the Relationship between Regime Change and the Culture of Politics." *African Studies Review* 37, no. 1 (1994): 39–67.

Rothchild, Donald. "The United States and Conflict Management in Africa," in *Africa in World Politics,* edited by Donald Rothchild and John Harbeson. 2d ed. Boulder: Westview, 1995.

Rothchild, Donald, and Caroline Hartzell. "The Case of Angola: Four Power Intervention and Disengagement," in *Foreign Military Intervention,* edited by Ariel E. Levite, Bruce W. Jentleson, and Larry Berman. New York: Columbia University Press, 1992.

Rothchild, Donald, and John Ravenhill. "Retreat from Globalism: U.S. Policy toward Africa in the 1990s," in *Eagle in a New World: American Grand Strategy in the Post–Cold War Era,* edited by Kenneth A. Oye, Robert J. Lieber, and Donald Rothchild. New York: HarperCollins, 1992.

Rupesinghe, Kumar, ed. *Conflict Resolution in Uganda.* Oslo: International Peace Research Institute/Ohio University Press, 1989.

Sahnoun, Mohamed. *Somalia: The Missed Opportunities.* Washington, D.C.: United States Institute of Peace Press, 1994.

Schraeder, Peter J. *United States Foreign Policy toward Africa: Incrementalism, Crisis, and Change.* New York: Cambridge University Press, 1994.

Sisk, Timothy D. *Democratization in South Africa: The Elusive Social Contract.* Princeton, N.J.: Princeton University Press, 1995.

Smock, David R., ed. *Making War and Waging Peace: Foreign Intervention in Africa.* Washington, D.C.: United States Institute of Peace Press, 1993.

Stedman, Stephen John. *Peacemaking in Civil Wars: International Mediation in Zimbabwe, 1974–1980.* Boulder: Lynne Rienner, 1990.

Wiseman, John A. *Democracy in Black Africa: Survival and Renewal.* New York: Paragon House, 1990.

CONTRIBUTORS

Herman J. Cohen is a retired foreign service officer who specialized in African affairs for most of his thirty-eight-year career. He served as senior director for Africa in the National Security Council, deputy director general of the Foreign Service, U.S. ambassador to Senegal and the Gambia, and several other posts. His last government position was assistant secretary of state for African affairs from 1989 to 1993. He was awarded the Senior Foreign Service Presidential Distinguished Rank Award in 1994. He is currently senior adviser to the Global Coalition for Africa, an intergovernmental policy forum concerned with economic development issues.

Chester A. Crocker is chairman of the Board of Directors of the United States Institute of Peace and distinguished research professor of diplomacy at the Georgetown University School of Foreign Service. In 1989–90, Crocker was a distinguished fellow in the Institute's Jennings Randolph Program for International Peace. While there, he began writing *High Noon in Southern Africa: Making Peace in a Rough Neighborhood.* From 1981 to 1989, Crocker was assistant secretary of state for African affairs. He was the principal diplomatic architect and mediator in the prolonged negotiations among Angola, Cuba, and South Africa that led to the withdrawal of Cuban troops from Angola and the independence of Namibia. Earlier, Crocker was on the Georgetown faculty and a staff member of the National Security Council. In addition to numerous articles for foreign policy journals, he is coeditor of *South Africa in the 1980s.*

B. A. Kiplagat has served as Kenyan ambassador to Britain and France, as well as permanent secretary of Kenya's Ministry of Foreign Affairs. He played a key role in the Mozambique peace process. He was earlier deputy executive director of the National Christian Council of Kenya. He is currently active in promoting peace in several African countries through cooperation with the All-Africa Conference of Churches and other organizations.

Ali A. Mazrui, a Kenyan, is Albert Schweitzer professor and director of the Institute of Global Cultural Studies, State University of New York at Binghamton. He is also Albert Luthuli professor-at-large, University of Jos, Nigeria, and senior scholar at Cornell University. He has published more than twenty books, including *Cultural Forces in World Politics* and *Africa since 1935* (coeditor). He is perhaps best known for his television series *The Africans: A Triple Heritage.*

Robert B. Oakley is a retired career foreign service officer. He served as U.S. ambassador to Somalia, Zaire, and Pakistan. More recently he served as the president's special envoy to Somalia during 1992–93. He previously directed the Special Initiative on the Middle East of the United States Institute of Peace. He is currently a visiting senior fellow at the National Defense University. He coauthored *Somalia and Operation Restore Hope: Reflections on Peacemaking and Peacekeeping.*

Donald Rothchild is professor of political science at the University of California, Davis. He is currently on leave, serving as peace fellow at the United States Institute of Peace. He has been a member of the faculty at universities in Uganda, Kenya, Zambia, and Ghana. His books include *Racial Bargaining in Independent Kenya; Scarcity, Choice, and Public Policy in Middle Africa* (coauthor); and *Politics and Society in Contemporary Africa* (coauthor). He is currently completing a book on ethnicity and conflict management in Africa.

Timothy D. Sisk is program officer in the grant program at the United States Institute of Peace. He specializes in comparative ethnic, racial, national, and religious conflict and conflict resolution. The author of *Democratization in South Africa: The Elusive Social Contract,* he has also written articles for scholarly journals on democratization in deeply divided societies, on African politics generally, and on South African politics specifically. From 1990 to 1991, Sisk was a Fulbright scholar in South Africa. He is an adjunct professor in the Liberal Studies Program at Georgetown University. During 1995 he is on a Nobel Institute fellowship in Oslo.

David R. Smock is director of the grant program of the United States Institute of Peace and coordinator of the Institute's activities on Africa.

Smock was a staff member of the Ford Foundation from 1964 to 1980, serving in Nigeria, Ghana, Kenya, and Lebanon, as well as in New York. From 1975 to 1980, he served as director of the South African Education Program, a scholarship program that brings black South African students to U.S. universities. During that time he was also vice president for program development and research for the Institute of International Education in New York. From 1986 to 1989, he was executive associate to the president of the United Church of Christ, after which he became executive director of International Voluntary Services, supervising development projects in Africa, Asia, and Latin America. Smock edited *Making War and Waging Peace: Foreign Intervention in Africa* and is author or editor of six other books, most of which are on African topics.

I. William Zartman is Jacob Blaustein professor of international organization and conflict resolution at the School of Advanced International Studies at Johns Hopkins University, as well as director of African studies. He was formerly a visiting fellow at the United States Institute of Peace and professor of political science at New York University. He has written numerous books on Africa, negotiation, and conflict resolution, including *Conflict Resolution in Africa* (coeditor), *International Crisis Management, The Practical Negotiator,* and *Ripe for Resolution: Conflict and Intervention in Africa.*

OTHER SYMPOSIUM PARTICIPANTS

Ambassador Jacques Bacamurwanko, former ambassador of Burundi to the United States

Dr. Pauline Baker, Georgetown University

Professor Gerald Bender, University of Southern California

Dr. Herschelle S. Challenor, Clark Atlanta University

Dr. Michael Chege, Harvard University

Ted Dagne, staff of House of Representatives Subcommittee on Africa

Ambassador Francis Deng, Brookings Institution

Barbara Gibson, Embassy of Canada

Dr. Harriet Hentges, United States Institute of Peace

Dr. Richard Joseph, Carter Center and Emory University

Professor Edmond Keller, University of California at Los Angeles

Reed Kramer, Africa News Service

Roger Laloupo, Economic Community of West African States

Dr. Michael Lund, United States Institute of Peace

Dr. Terrence Lyons, Brookings Institution

Lt. Col. Anthony D. Marley, State Department

Aileen Marshall, Global Coalition for Africa

Professor Guy Martin, Clark Atlanta University

Ambassador Olara A. Otunnu, International Peace Academy

Carolyn Reynolds, Interaction

Ambassador David Shinn, State Department

Peter Shiras, Interaction

John Sommer, Refugee Policy Group

Professor Stephen Stedman, School of Advanced International Studies, Johns Hopkins University

Professor Scott Thompson, Fletcher School, Tufts University, and board member, United States Institute of Peace

Ambassador Melissa Wells, State Department

James Woods, formerly deputy assistant secretary for African Affairs, Defense Department

Andrea Young, House of Representatives staff

Professor Crawford Young, University of Wisconsin

INDEX

AACC. *See* All-Africa Conference of Churches
AAS. *See* African Academy of Sciences
Abacha military regime, 71
Abiola, Chief, 71
Abuja peace process, 46
Addis Ababa Accords, 15, 33, 42–43
Adoula, Cyrille, 60, 61
Africa. *See also specific regions and states by name*
  boundary demarcation, 102–103, 112
  capacity-building, 98–99, 105–120, 127–128
  conflict management capabilities, 77–94
  democratization, 32, 102, 112–114
  disarmament and demobilization, 99
  failed-state syndrome, 113–114
  heads of state summit, 1994, 88
  needs and desires, 87–88
  as political refugee, 9–25
  rebuilding structures, 99–100
  "second independence," 106
  standards for dealing with conflict, 97
  willingness to work with international community to resolve conflicts, 79–80
Africa Confidential, 2–3
Africa Leadership Forum, 7

African Academy of Sciences
  working group to address Africa's internal conflicts, 35
African Conflict Resolution Act, 7, 118, 128
African Leadership Forum, 109
African National Congress
  accession to power, 35
African Peace Corps proposal, 110
African Peace Fund, 6
African security council proposal, 22–23, 108–109
"African solutions to African problems" principle, 2
African state as political refugee metaphor, 9–10
Africa Reconciliation, 8
Aideed, Mohamed Farah, 4, 35, 49, 69
Ajello, Aldo, 129–130
Albright, Madeleine, 5
Algeria, 102
  dual society in, 16
  inability to control territory, 114
Alienation issue, 9
All-Africa Conference of Churches
  magnitude of demands on, 34
  role in Addis Ababa agreement, 33
  role in Sudan, 34
  as truly regional NGO, 114–115
Anarchy. *See* Tyranny-anarchy dilemma